Powerful
Telephone Skills

A Guide to Effective
Communication

BARNES & NOBLE BOOKS
NEW YORK

2004 Barnes & Noble Books

ISBN 0-7607-4554-4

Printed and bound in the United States of America

04 05 06 07 08 09 M 9 8 7 6 5 4 3 2 1

TABLE of CONTENTS

Introduction

INTRODUCTION

The telephone is the most pervasive communication tool in business today. In fact, every day approximately 500 million telephone calls are transacted.

Consequently, millions of businesses project their images and reputations through the telephone lines daily. Customers are won and lost between the second and third unanswered rings, within the chasm called "hold," by an interminable transfer and the sneer or smile of a voice. How we conduct business over the telephone can make or break our company. Our manner must be both professional and personal to address the needs of a customer in a high-tech, global society.

While we depend on the telephone as our primary communication tool, it also produces long-winded callers, disconnected lines, unanswered messages and, ultimately, a lot of frustration. The miscommunication that often results leaves us feeling that the telephone is not the "perfect" tool Alexander Graham Bell described. Since the first telephone call in 1886, we've wrestled with the aggravation of telephone miscommunication despite giant leaps in technology that have made the telephone virtually a minicomputer.

Clearly, we will become even more dependent on the telephone in the next century, and with each new decade will come challenges and changes.

Our telephone style, telemarketing strategy and communication skills must be effective to withstand the stresses of business today and tomorrow. Taking the time now to develop techniques for answering calls, marketing products and services, listening between the sentences, qualifying customers, satisfying needs, ensuring return business and recording efficient messages will assuredly save you time — and customers — later.

This handbook helps you cope with the problems and frustrations you encounter and shows you how to refine your telephone skills to become more effective and productive.

YOUR TELEPHONE IMAGE

Communicating effectively on the telephone is a unique skill, and when mastered, it can make you very successful. Learning to communicate professionally and effectively on the telephone is within your grasp. It is a skill that can be mastered with just a little practice.

This handbook covers the basics of effective telephone communication. Emphasized throughout are the following key elements:

- Listening skills
- Professional and precise communication
- Techniques for handling difficult situations and people
- Controlling telephone conversations
- Creating positive images for ourselves and the companies we represent

Let's first look at ways you can make a positive impression on people who call you or others in your company.

Make a Positive Impression

Even though most of us hate to admit it, we form impressions of people quickly. Usually within two minutes we've decided if we like them and — if we have a choice — whether we want to continue the relationship.

Like it or not, this is also true when we talk to people on the telephone. And, more importantly, not only do we make judgments about the people we speak with, but they also evaluate us. Sales people, customer service agents and switchboard operators are the first-line representatives of your companies. Those of you in these positions must be mindful of the impressions you project.

Each of us has the ability to make positive or negative impressions on the people we talk to on the telephone each day. In many cases, the impression you give callers influences how they feel about your company. More than 500 *million* phone calls are made each day. Each call is an opportunity for us to make a positive impact.

Creating a positive impression with callers comes naturally to all of us some days...when we are in a good mood, enthusiastic about our jobs or dealing with a familiar, friendly voice. The key is to make positive impressions *consistently* so callers form the same positive impression of your company. This requires certain habits that aren't affected by the kind of day you have.

1. **Be on Stage.**
   Actors have to perform whether they have a good day or bad day. Granted, some performances are more outstanding than others, but even the worst performances should still leave the audience feeling satisfied.

   The same holds true for your telephone conversations. You can keep your personal feelings and moods separate from your professional demeanor if you view your time on the telephone as being on stage.

Regardless of your job, you know the role you should play: receptionist/goodwill ambassador, customer service/problem solver, public relations representative, etc. Learn to assume that role automatically, regardless of your personal feelings.

2. **Practice Consistency.**
Consistency is crucial to establishing and maintaining a good impression. Whether you screen telephone calls or route them in your company, keep your salutation and any follow-up questions consistent.

3. **Critique Yourself.**
Get friends (or friends of friends whose voices you don't recognize) to call you. Then have them give you feedback on the impression they got. Can you improve how you answer the telephone? The questions you ask? Your tone of voice? Your grammar? Ask them what overall impressions they formed from what they heard.

4. **Use Role Models.** —Keisha
If you have a job that requires extensive use of the telephone or if you want to improve your telephone image, find a good role model. This can be a colleague or someone you have talked with on the telephone who demonstrates excellent communication skills. Listen carefully to all aspects of how the model handles a conversation. Study the style and techniques, then adapt them, where possible, to your job.

5. **Answer the Phone Promptly.** —2 ring max
Avoid letting the telephone ring more than three or four times. Answering promptly conveys a strong message that you and your business are more efficient.

6. **Minimize "Hold" Time.**
One of the most frustrating things for any caller is to be put on hold for an extended period of time. If you can't find the person the caller is trying to reach or if that person is on

another line, check back with the caller every minute or so to find out if he or she wants to continue holding or leave a message.

7. **Give the Caller Adjustment Time.**
Our ears are very sensitive to sound, and on the phone it takes 10 to 30 seconds to adjust to voices. Give the caller a chance to absorb your vocal qualities before you begin your salutation. Make a habit of saying, "Good morning," or "Good afternoon." This gives the caller time to adjust to your voice before going on to the most important part of your greeting.

If the caller isn't given this adjustment period, he or she may not retain the information you give. He or she may hear it, but won't absorb it.

8. **Announce Your Name.**
Most customer service experts advise that you give your name to callers. This shows a willingness to help. However, if you are not the person who will provide assistance, giving your name can be time-consuming and confusing.

If you will be following up with the caller to answer a question or provide more information, be sure to give your name.

When you announce your name, state how you want to be addressed: "Mr. Jones," "Ms. Scott," etc. Use a more formal approach if you want to convey a sense of authority. If you give both your first and last names (Bill Jones or Margaret Scott), you are more likely to be treated informally.

These techniques are the foundation for the professional telephone skills we will discuss in subsequent chapters.

Improve Your Telephone Style

If you have a role model, you probably recognize that this person has a telephone "style" that allows him or her to effectively communicate and make others feel comfortable. You may have already identified the elements of your role model's style that contribute to his or her success. If not, the following are important aspects of telephone style that you need to practice.

1. **Speak Conversationally.**
   A conversational tone can improve your effectiveness on the telephone, both as a listener and as a persuader. It is extremely important that you make your voice pleasant and eager and that you make each caller (or person you call) believe that he or she is the sole focus of your attention. Even if you speak with 800 people a day, the intimate and caring tone in your voice makes the difference in the other party's attitude toward you and your organization.

   As a listener, you should be conscious of the tonal qualities of the other party. Many people are uncomfortable saying "no" when you ask, "Is this a good time to talk?" So they grudgingly let the conversation continue. Listen closely to how they respond to the conversation. Are they relaxed? Participating in the conversation? Or do they seem distracted? Impatient?

   Give them alternatives if you initiated the call. Instead of asking a question that requires a "yes" or "no" response, give them a choice such as, "Is this a convenient time for you, or may I call back at 3 p.m.?" Don't say, "Should I call back later?" Be specific in the option you give. If they choose to reschedule the conversation, be sure to be prompt in returning the call.

2. Monitor Your Voice Tone.

Tone of voice is a truthful indicator of the mood we are in. Often, other people are more aware of our mood than we are because they hear our voices differently than we do.

As you listen to the tone of voice, focus on the pitch. In normal conversation, we use only a few "notes" in our speaking range. If you use a wide range of pitches or tones as you speak, your language appears more colorful. This use of ranges must come naturally to you or it will sound contrived. You can evaluate your speaking tone by taping your voice in routine conversations on the telephone.

Here are some voice tones and what they say to the listener:

- FLAT .... Bored, lack of interest in job
- INDIFFERENT ...... Not interested in caller or conversation
- ENTHUSIASTIC ... Interested in the conversation, likes job, interested in helping caller
- CARING .... Interested in the caller, anxious to help.
- COLD .... Hostile

The fastest way to improve your voice tone is to smile as you speak. The listener can't see it, but he or she can hear it.

3. Assess Your Voice Quality.

Like your tone of voice, your voice quality creates an image in the listener's mind. Think of how you perceive two different voices: one that is full and resonant and another that is shrill and nasal. You probably have a more positive image of the former.

A woman who has a breathy, "sexy" voice may impress some people, but to many she is not taken seriously in a business environment. She is probably not the person a client or customer trusts to solve a shipping problem, straighten out a billing error or negotiate the best price with a vendor.

Generally, we are not aware of our voice quality. We tend to adjust our voice to different situations. When we speak to friends or family members, our voices take on a lighter, more intimate quality. When we are angry or serious, they take on a deeper, louder sound.

These variations are normal for everyone. The key is learning to match your voice quality to your situation and words. It is inappropriate to be light and giddy when talking to a customer who calls with a complaint. It is appropriate to have a well-modulated, professional tone that conveys concern, efficiency and a desire to get the matter resolved promptly.

To assess your voice quality, tape record yourself as you speak in different situations — with customers, clients, fellow employees, friends and family members. Think of how you would react to your voice if you were the listener. Double check your assessment by having friends or co-workers listen to the tape and give you their reaction.

Finally, listen closely to the voice quality of people you admire, such as customers, co-workers, your boss, television reporters, and radio announcers. The common quality they should all have is that they are effective communicators. Study the way they modulate their voice quality and learn from it.

2

ANSWERING CALLS

Answering calls diplomatically may be the single most important task of any business. Studies show that seven out of 10 potential customers decide not to use a business after their first call because the line was not answered fast enough or cheerfully enough. Tips for handling customer service calls, for screening calls and for dealing with demanding callers are included in this chapter.

Customer Service

Although it may not produce direct sales, the customer service department can be one of the most important departments in a business. Several statistics bear mentioning here. Studies show that 15 to 20 percent of all responses to an 800 number are complaints, and half of those people never buy from that company again. That's a loss of seven-and-a-half to 10 percent of the customer base. Furthermore, each unhappy customer tells approximately 26 other people about his or her dissatisfaction. However, these same studies show that half of those who complain would buy again if their complaints were handled quickly. It costs five times more to get a new customer than to keep an existing one. Your role as a customer service representative is just as important to your company's bottom line as that of a salesperson. The receptionist or secretary who initially answers the phone is the first customer service representative that the caller encounters. It is essential that the representative know how to control the conversation in order to control the caller's impression of the company as well as the time spent on the telephone.

It is important, however, for callers to feel a sense of participation — not that they are being controlled or pushed around. Controlling the conversation involves not only practicing the following techniques but also knowing how to apply them subtly and effectively.

1. **Ask Questions.**
   You should ask questions for these reasons:

   - To gain information
   - To focus the conversation
   - To gain consensus when necessary
   - To begin the closure process

   Asking questions can be compared to firing a rifle. You take aim, then "fire" a question. Your aim is what you want the conversation to focus on. Firing the question gets the caller to address that focus.

   Questions also lead callers to believe they are in control because you have taken the time to ask them for their opinion or information. The caller feels important, yet you are in control.

2. **Give Callers Options.**
   Giving callers options does two things: It gives you the opportunity to control their responses, and it leads them to believe they are participating and have choices.

Child psychologists have known this to be an effective tactic for years. Never tell children they have to eat a vegetable; instead, give them a choice: peas or corn? Children rarely want to eat vegetables, but at least they feel in control of their options.

Here are some options you can offer callers:

- "Would you like to leave a message or hold?"
- "Would you rather I transfer you to customer service or take your name and number and have Mr. Anderson return your call?"
- "Is a 10:45 a.m. or a 2:45 p.m. appointment better for you?"
- "Do you prefer to pay by credit card or direct billing?"

3. **Tell Callers What You Are Going to Do.**
We've all felt helpless on the telephone when we've been put on hold indefinitely or transferred to three departments and still not talked to the right person.

When we do this to callers, we are telling them they have no choice and certainly no control over the situation. These feelings produce frustration and a negative impression of you and your company. One way to avoid this is to tell callers what you are going to do *before* you do it.

When transferring callers to another department, give them the name of the department and the person you are connecting them with. If you need to place callers on hold, tell them so and ask if that's acceptable. Finally, inform callers. If you have trouble finding the person they are trying to reach, explain the situation diplomatically, then give them options.

4. **Know Your Resources**
You can be in control of your telephone conversations only if you can respond to a wide variety of requests, problems and

challenges. One of the worst things you can convey to a caller is ignorance.

Knowledge of your company — its departments, products or services and the roles of people within each department — is invaluable for exercising maximum control over your telephone conversations. This knowledge allows you the greatest number of choices in dealing with problems and requests. These choices translate into options you can give the caller, which means you demonstrate your expertise and provide a valuable service.

Take the time to become familiar with your company. The greater your knowledge, the greater your control.

Types of Calls

Now that you see how important you can be, you need to be aware of what types of calls you can receive. The calls you will handle fall into one of six categories.

1. **Answering Complaints**
   One out of five incoming calls is a complaint. However, most customers don't air their complaints for one of two reasons.

   • They don't know where or whom to complain to.
   • They don't think it will help to complain.

2. **Dealing With Requests for General Information**
   This type of call comes in as often as a complaint does. If a customer calls with a general question and has it answered quickly and politely, the perception of added value is increased. This may also give your customer new ideas on how to use your product and thereby increase sales.

3. **Handling Questions About Billing**
   Although these questions sometimes take a little longer to resolve, they pay dividends. If your customer has a question or dispute, he or she probably won't pay the bill until it's resolved. The customer's irritation will also increase, which he or she will share with other people. The faster the problem is resolved, the faster your company gets paid. As a bonus, the customer is satisfied.

4. **Answering Inquiries About Service or Warranties**
   In numerous surveys of why customers buy, service and warranties always rank at or near the top. In most cases, these are even more important than the price. When you resolve these questions in a quick and efficient manner, you reinforce one of your customers' major reasons for buying.

5. **Answering Questions on Use**
   This is very similar to answering questions on service. If your customers don't know how to use your product, not only will they not buy it again, but they will also tell others not to buy it because it's too difficult to operate. In many cases, the questions are simple to answer.

6. **Handling Inquiries on New Business**
   This can, and usually does, lead to new sales. By referring your customer/prospect to the right people, or by answering his or her questions on opening a new account, you make the decision to start or expand with your company a very easy one.

Objectives

The more quickly you can determine what type of call you've received, the more quickly you can resolve your customer's problem. To do your job effectively, you need to keep two major objectives in mind:

1. You need to react to your incoming call in a quick and efficient manner.

2. You need to get as much information about your customer as possible. This information can help prevent future problems.

Telephone Tips

Identifying calls and knowing your objectives are only part of being successful in customer service. There are certain techniques you can use to improve your effectiveness. Here are some tips to consider:

1. **Answer Your Phone Promptly.**
   Your customer is calling with a concern. The longer your phone rings, the more his or her concern grows. Answering quickly stops this feeling from getting out of control, and it also portrays you as quick and efficient.

2. **Identify Yourself and Your Company Immediately.**
   In addition to being the polite way of answering a call, it's also a means of confirming to your customer that he or she has reached the desired person and/or place.

3. **Be Friendly.**
Always start with a friendly, helpful attitude. It offsets many negative feelings before they have a chance to worsen. In addition, it sends a message of concern and warmth to your customer.

4. **Have All Your Necessary Resources Available.**
When someone is calling with a problem or concern, the last thing he or she wants to do is wait for you to get ready. In addition to inflaming a potentially tense situation, this also gives the image of your being unorganized and incompetent. Obviously, this is not the image you want to create with someone who is depending on you to resolve a problem. Make sure you have price lists, technical specifications and other pertinent information at your fingertips.

5. **Indicate Your Regret or Appreciation When Applicable.**
There are times when your customer wants reinforcement from you. It may be due to frustration with his or her problem, or it may be complimenting something you or your company did well. Since the customer can't see you, he or she has to be reinforced verbally. It is easy to recognize good news, but situations requiring expressions of regret are harder to identify. Here are some guidelines for when to express regret:

- If your customer mentions something personal (Example: "I've been sick for two weeks.")
- If your customer was disconnected on an earlier call
- If a commitment made by your company was not honored because of a broken promise or a missed due date
- If your customer claims someone in your company made a mistake (whether it's true or not)
- If your customer has been on hold for more than a minute

6. **Use the Caller's Name If It's Offered.**
A person's name is magic. This technique puts the call on a less threatening, more informed basis.

7. **Express Your Willingness to Help.**
Just providing information itself is not good enough. Letting your customer know you want to help distinguishes you from the competition and serves as a great positive first impression.

8. **Don't Interrupt Your Customer.**
We all miss some details in any conversation. The important thing to remember is to confirm your information when your customer gives you an opportunity. Interrupting a customer in mid-sentence sends several messages:

   • You're not polite or sensitive to feelings, and therefore, you may not be sensitive to business needs.
   • You are not listening to what he or she is saying, which may be a critical piece of information.
   • You may have missed other important information.

Either way, you lose. Wait until your customer quits talking; then get the information you missed.

9. **Get As Much Information As You Can.**
Remember, this is one of your key objectives. If you are on a mechanized system that requires information to access other files, obtain it quickly. Ask for it early in the conversation. Your customer's account number, telephone number or account name may be the key that gives you all other necessary information. You may also want to ask for several things in one question. It saves time. For example, "May I have your name, address and telephone number, please?"

10. **Be Understandable in Your Communication.**
Take precautions to ensure that you speak clearly. It's a tremendous waste to resolve a problem for your customer and then have the solution delayed because of poor

communication skills. Develop good verbal and written skills.

11. **Be Accurate and Complete When Giving Information.**
Make sure you give accurate information in a prompt manner. If you are unsure or don't know something, say so. Your customer will be much better served and far more pleased if you say something like, "I'm not sure, but I'll find out and get back to you in _____ minutes." If you can clear up the question in 60 seconds or so, it's acceptable to put your customer on hold, providing he or she agrees. Also, avoid terms such as "I think," "possibly" and "maybe." These destroy confidence in you.

12. **Be Easy to Deal With.**
Be professional in both the function of your job and in your attitude. Identify exactly what type of call it is and decide as quickly as possible how you can help. You're there to help your customer as quickly and accurately as possible. Make certain your customer knows this. Also, be careful not to utter negative, profane or meaningless comments. These have a tendency to create negative feelings in your customer. Be helpful, efficient, positive and firm. You need to convey four important points to your customer:

- He or she is doing you a favor by calling, and you want to improve your business.
- You are a good listener and are sympathetic to his or her problem.
- You understand your business and what he or she needs.
- You will resolve his or her problem quickly and efficiently.

13. **Transfer Calls Only When You Have To.**
Try to resolve your customer's problem by yourself if possible. However, there are times when it is necessary to

involve another person or department, or the customer may have called the wrong person. When you have to transfer, use these guidelines:

- Explain that you need to transfer your customer and why. For example, "Mrs. Morey helps our Kansas customers. I'll be happy to transfer you."
- Make sure your customer does not mind being transferred. If the customer doesn't want to be transferred for whatever reason, offer to get the information necessary to help and call back.
- If the customer doesn't mind being transferred, proceed. There are two things you need to do here. First, say you are transferring the call, but in case it gets disconnected, give the customer the number he or she needs to reach and the person's name, if applicable. Second, stay on the line until the desired employee answers. Introduce your customer, briefly explain the problem and disconnect from the conversation.

14. **Hang Up Gently.**
Last, but not least, make sure you hang up gently. Regardless of how well you've done on the call, if the last thing your customer hears is a receiver slammed down on the cradle, then the conversation has ended on a negative note. Don't ruin it here.

There are industry-specific tips you may use on your job. If you follow these good techniques, your customer service will improve dramatically.

Format for Answering Calls

Every call from your customer has to be handled on an individual basis since each problem or inquiry is unique, at least to your customer. We will combine the calls mentioned earlier into two basic types: requesting information and complaining about something. Following are ways to handle these types of calls:

Information Requests
- *Identify yourself* and your company or department.
- *Record, confirm and repeat the request.* You need to make sure your customer knows you have his or her request. Nothing is more frustrating than silence when you want a question answered.
- *Express your willingness to help.* Start the call off on a positive note. It eliminates potential problems.
- *Restate the question.* The only thing worse than silence is to answer a question or inquiry that your customer didn't ask. Make sure both of you are in agreement about the need.
- *Answer the question or inquiry.* Remember, do this in a friendly, efficient and prompt manner.
- *Conclude the call.* When you conclude the call, confirm that you have given your customer the information he or she needs. Last, make sure you leave your customer with a warm, friendly closing statement. Reiterate your availability to help with future requests for information.

Complaints
- *Identify yourself* and your company or department.
- *Record the type of complaint.* This may mean being quiet while your customer "blows off" steam.
- *Restate the information and the problem* he or she gave you. Do this briefly, but indicate you know what the problem really is.
- *Express regret and a willingness to help.* Here more than anywhere else, your customer needs to know that you understand and want to help.
- *Resolve the problem.* This may not be possible in every call, but this is your objective. If a call-back is necessary, do so. Confirm all your actions with your customer so he or she knows you're working to resolve the problem.

• *Conclude the call.* As with information calls, make sure you confirm that the original problem is resolved to your customer's satisfaction. Leave your customer with a helpful, warm closing statement and the offer to provide future help if necessary.

Screening Calls

Let's face it. Screening calls is difficult. But it doesn't have to be impossible or uncomfortable. As the person answering the telephone, you are in the position to establish the tone of the conversation.

Consider the dynamics of the situation: In the eyes of callers, you are the barrier standing between them and whomever they are calling. The caller's objective is to overcome that barrier and talk to the person you protect. Your job, however, is to protect the privacy of the people you screen calls for and prevent unnecessary interruptions. At the same time, you are expected to project a positive image to customers and clients.

Screening calls is often perceived as difficult because, in many ways, your job is at odds with the caller's objectives. But there are ways to screen calls diplomatically. Here are several steps you can take to avoid confrontations, maintain a positive image and still do your job effectively:

1. **Explain Why You Ask Questions.**
   Why screen calls? To make people angry? To make them think you're suspicious? Of course not, but that's the impression many callers get when they are asked questions regarding their names and the companies they represent. One way to eliminate negative reactions to questions is to tell the caller why you need the information. For example, you might say:

- "Mr. Jones, I need your name and number so I can give my supervisor the correct information."
- "Ms. Johnson, my supervisor needs your company's name and the account number so she can retrieve the information on your account."

Explaining the reasons for your questions helps overcome the caller's suspicion.

2. **Practice Being a "Broken Record."**
   When you speak to someone who won't cooperate or who tries to tell you something you know is incorrect, use the "broken record" technique.

   For instance, a caller wants your boss to return a phone call. You ask for his or her name, organization and telephone number. He or she replies, "Just tell him Bill called." You know your boss knows at least five "Bills," so you respond, "...and your last name and telephone number?" He or she responds in irritation, "He knows who I am."

   Now you can use the broken record technique. Your objective is to get the necessary information. Avoid a confrontation by ignoring his or her irritation and politely ask, "Just in case, I need your last name and telephone number, please." He or she responds, "Didn't you hear me? He knows me. Just tell him I called."

   This is where conversations often turn ugly. By using the broken record technique, however, you stay focused on the information you need, not the caller's attitude. If appropriate, you can appeal to the caller's desire to meet his or her objective – talking to your boss. You respond: "Sir, my boss knows many people and it helps him or her return calls promptly if there are last names and telephone numbers." The caller sighs, "Okay, the last name is Powell, and my number is 476-7676. Have him (or her) call me as soon as possible."

Your next response is critical. How you close the conversation has an enormous impact on how the caller perceives the exchange and the image of your company. You respond, "Thank you for calling, Mr. Powell. I will give my boss the message. I appreciate your time today. Good-bye."

3. Let Them Hear You Smile.
While what you say is critical, more important is your tone of voice. Callers will be irritated by a tone that is indifferent, hostile or too reserved.

Smile when you screen calls. It may sound silly, but if you smile, callers hear it. They are more inclined to perceive you as helpful and friendly. In addition to giving the caller a good impression, a smile boosts your confidence.

4. Know What Information You Need From Callers.
Write down standard questions you ask each caller and refer to these when you are on the telephone. Be consistent. Callers who become familiar with your questions are more likely to cooperate if they understand this is fundamental information you ask everyone.

Your standard questioning might go something like this:

- Company identification and salutation
- Ask the caller his or her name/organization
- Ask the caller to whom he or she wants to speak
- Give the appropriate response

Get into the habit of asking callers for their names/ organizations first, instead of the person they seek. This greatly minimizes their feelings of being screened. Ask questions with confidence and authority. If your voice sounds tentative, callers perceive this immediately and respond accordingly. If you ask questions professionally and expect an answer, you will be successful.

5. **Volunteer Your Knowledge/Expertise.**
   Callers feel less frustrated if they think you are genuinely interested in helping them. Assert yourself and ask callers if there's anything you can help them with. Often callers volunteer information if you volunteer action.

   Don't hesitate to volunteer your knowledge and expertise. Handle the situation in one of these ways:

   - "Ms. Blake, my boss is not available at the moment. However, I assist with the direct mail project and am familiar with your account. Perhaps I can answer your questions?"
   - "Mr. Blake, I've assisted Mr. Bailey for three years and am very familiar with our operation. May I answer a question for you?"

6. **Think About What You Say and What They Hear.**
   Think about the initial responses you give to callers and the impressions that are created. Do you say these not-so-positive statements?

   - "She's not in yet."
   - "He's in a meeting."
   - "She's still at lunch."
   - "I don't know when he'll be back."

   In your mind you are stating facts, but the caller formulates negative perceptions. Let's compare what you say to what the caller hears, then look at alternative responses.

When You Say This:	The Caller Thinks:	So Try This:
"He's not in yet."	"What's wrong with this guy? Can't he get to to work by 9 a.m.?"	"Mr. Jones had an early meeting, but I expect him at 11 a.m. May I have him call you?"
"He's in a meeting."	"You are just trying to give me the run-around."	"Mr. Jones is in a meeting until noon and then has a lunch meeting. May I have him call you this afternoon?"
"She's still at lunch."	"It's 2:30 p.m.! I wish I could take two hours hours for lunch. No wonder their fees are high!"	"Ms. Jones had a meeting with a client, and I expect her in after 2:45 p.m."
"I don't know when he'll be back."	"Nobody knows what's going on in that organization!"	"Mr. Jones will be out of the office most of the afternoon, but I will be glad to give him your message when he calls in."

It's important to realize that every statement you make creates an impression on the caller. If callers feel your responses are dishonest, insincere or rude, they remember them. In fact, once a negative impression is made, it takes many more positive transactions to "erase" the initial negative one.

Remember, give the caller an option when you answer the question. This way you can receive the response you want.

Screening calls is a demanding task. It requires time management, organization and people skills. Handling the demanding caller requires the same skills. Two of the most tiresome callers are the long-winded caller and the angry caller.

The Long-Winded Caller

Everyone loves an audience. And because it's rare to find someone who will listen in this fast-paced society, it is not uncommon to monopolize people's time on the telephone. Idle chitchat sometimes provides us with a break from a hectic day; other times it combats loneliness.

In any case, when people call and monopolize an unreasonable amount of your time, they become "long-winded callers." The sad fact is that these people often don't realize how they inconvenience others. Their rambling explanations and casual chatter become ingrained habits. The bottom line is that long-winded callers won't go away on their own. To deal effectively with them, we need to implement specific strategies to maintain control over our telephone time.

There are many different theories on how to deal with long-winded callers. Some telephone professionals believe that if you remain silent or give short, one-word answers, long-winded callers will realize you don't have time for the conversation. In reality, most people interpret little or no response from a listener as an indication of interest. Silence on the telephone is like a vacuum: it demands to be filled. So if you don't respond, the caller will keep talking.

Dealing with long-winded callers is not easy, but it isn't impossible. Here are five ways you can effectively control conversations with these callers:

1. Ask Questions.

Most long-winded callers don't know they are long-winded. In fact, most think they are being perfectly clear. Because they don't realize they take so much of your time and energy, you need to control the conversation in a way that lets them know you are interested in them and the subject. This still allows you to end the conversation at your discretion.

Ask leading questions to focus their thoughts and work toward conclusions. For example, you might begin like this:

- "Don't you think, Mr. Blake, that...?"
- "Isn't it true...?"
- "What if we begin the project in this manner...?"

These questions are designed to focus the caller's attention and response on the subject at hand.

Don't be afraid to interrupt long-winded callers with a question. They won't be offended as long as you appear interested in their responses. Use their responses to move toward a conclusion. If you need to accelerate this process, you can ask a direct question such as, "If you could phrase this information as a question, what would you ask me?"

2. Set the Course of the Conversation.

If you initiate a call to a customer who is long-winded or has difficulty sticking to the subject, it is vital that you establish the direction of the conversation at the beginning. This provides the listener with a clear road map and gives you a reference point if you encounter unnecessary diversions.

Use the following statements to establish a road map:

- "Mr. Smith, I need to ask you three questions concerning the status of your account...."
- "Ms. Green, I understand you are interested in our products. Let me take a few minutes to describe them to you...."

By laying the groundwork you control the conversation.

3. **Use the PRC Technique.**
   The PRC technique controls the conversation with three simple steps: paraphrase, reflect and close.

   PARAPHRASE: When the caller begins to talk in circles, you need to interrupt and say:

   "I need to make sure I understand what you've said...."

   At this point, you can paraphrase the important things the caller said. This ensures that you both understand the key points, and the caller is reassured that you have heard him or her.

   REFLECT: After you summarize the conversation, give callers a chance to respond to or "reflect" on what you've said. In essence, you allow them to agree or disagree and add anything you may have left out. If what they say seems inconclusive, you may want to probe their responses with an open-ended question:

   "John, what else can we do to solve the problem?"

   CLOSE: Once callers appear satisfied with your summary, then you must "close" the conversation. Begin by expressing appreciation for their time, or mention how happy you are about the outcome of the call. Be sure to mention any action you agreed on; then end the conversation.

4. Budget Time to Listen.

Often callers are long-winded because they are lonely and need someone to talk to. In this situation you can get stuck listening to stories about their weekend, their kids who won't talk to them, hospital stays and illnesses, and on and on.

How do you balance their need to talk with your desire to manage your time efficiently? Budget your listening time. When you talk to a customer, you have two conflicting desires: to create a positive image of your organization and to get off the telephone in a reasonable time frame. You can achieve both by investing a specific amount of time listening. Budget three to five minutes or whatever you can afford, but be sure to set a limit. Don't reveal this limit to the caller. As the end of that time period approaches, give the caller feedback that indicates you've heard what he or she has said, then conclude the conversation.

5. Establish Mutual Time Limits.

When you pick up the telephone and realize that the caller is long-winded, take control of the conversation before it begins. Tell the caller how much time you have to talk, then give him or her options. For instance, say:

> "It's good to hear from you, Steve. I'm leaving for a meeting in five minutes. Can we cover what you need now, or may I call you back?"

Finally, one of the most important elements for controlling a long-winded caller is patience. While giving a caller an additional minute or two seems impossible on some days, it is usually better to use these techniques for ending a conversation than to be abrupt or rude. Remember, your personal image as well as that of your company is always at stake.

The Angry Caller

Think about the last time you talked or tried to talk to an angry caller. Was the caller angry at you? Or were you just the unfortunate one who picked up the telephone? Chances are, they were not angry with you personally or even your organization. Some outside source triggered their negative feelings. Because callers sometimes have misplaced aggressions, you need to learn methods that effectively defuse their anger.

The first and most difficult step is to detach yourself from the hostility you encounter. While you may understand that the caller isn't upset with you personally, it is still hard not to react defensively to his or her negative attitude.

To maintain control of yourself and the situation, you must view it objectively and remain professional.

Here are some techniques you can use to maintain control.

1. **Let Callers Vent Their Anger.**
   The fastest way to defuse angry callers is to let them "blow off" steam. Don't interrupt. Let them talk and get whatever is bothering them off their chests. Remember, it takes two to sustain a conflict. If you respond to specific points, then they have engaged you in an argument. Wait. Hear them out.

   Understand the dynamics of the situation. The caller probably is upset by something else in his or her life and is taking it out on you. Frequently, it is easier to vent anger at a stranger, and particularly a faceless voice on the telephone, than deal directly with the person or situation that upset you.

   One of the most thankless jobs is taking complaint calls in an organization. Many callers respond to a problem, such as not receiving their evening newspaper, with far more hostility than is warranted because it gives them an opportunity to flush out the frustrations that have built up during the day. This is called "misplaced anger" or the "kick-the-dog" syndrome.

Most callers who speak in an angry tirade do this. They "kick the dog," and the dog happens to be you. Allow them to vent their anger by listening, not responding. Let them say whatever they want. If you respond, it will probably be seen as a rebuttal. The caller thinks you disagree with him or her. This only escalates an angry situation.

Some telephone professionals think this venting process is too time consuming. What's your alternative? Angry callers usually take a lot of your time because you have to try to pacify them or come up with solutions that benefit both of you. However, until callers get the anger out, they won't want to listen to rational solutions. The next time you confront a difficult caller, give this a try. Don't say anything except perhaps, "I understand," until you hear silence on the other end. Then try these suggestions:

Indicate You Heard Them.
A good listener is a rarity. Being a patient and effective listener helps pacify angry callers, but only if they feel you have heard their grievances. So when they stop talking, start giving feedback to indicate you heard the key points. You don't have to agree or endorse their complaints, just summarize.

Be on Their Side.
Even if the caller is wrong (and those of you in customer service know this *never* happens!), empathize with him or her. Often callers don't expect you to solve their problems as much as they want you to listen to them.

Call the Person by Name.
This sounds like a small point, but whenever possible,

use the caller's name. This personalizes the conversation and makes it difficult for the caller to attack you.

Listen for Unspoken Messages.
Along with hearing the verbal message, take time to listen for messages that are not stated overtly. All of us speak on two levels: the verbal and the non-verbal. Because we don't have the ability to analyze clues such as body language or facial expression over the phone, we must focus on the subtleties of the caller's voice — inflection, pacing of words and the overall tension level.

Being in tune with these messages helps you hear what the caller says on all levels. It also helps determine when the caller is ready to listen to solutions and alternatives.

2. **Respond Professionally.**
Remember, the key is not to take the anger personally — take it professionally. Recognize that callers may have legitimate concerns. They may be overreacting to the problem, but don't let that cloud your ability to objectively assess the problem and its solution. Until you can offer some specific action, here are responses that can help you deal with hostile callers.

- "We apologize for that oversight, Mr. Jones." (Apologize only when you or the organization is at fault.)
- "We regret that inclement weather forces us to cancel the engagement." (Express regret even when something happened over which you or the organization had no control.)
- "We will do everything we can to change the situation for you." (This does not obligate you to do what the caller demands.)
- "Thank you for bringing this to our attention. It's customers like you who help us improve our service."

3. **Out of Sight, Out of Mind.**
It is extremely unhealthy for telephone professionals to let an angry caller ruin their day. This produces a negative ripple effect:

- It makes it more difficult to deal enthusiastically with subsequent callers.
- It affects your overall attitude toward your job, your boss, your company and fellow employees.
- It reduces your efficiency because you focus on healing your emotional wounds rather than on your job.

Telephones have a magical quality. When you hang up, you disconnect yourself from the angry caller. (Don't hang up on these people prematurely, though!) The anger and hostility become history. They are gone from your life. When callers say "good-bye," they're gone. You can go on to the next caller and hope for a more pleasant conversation.

When you deal with angry callers, do everything you can to help them. When the transaction is complete, move on to the next challenge.

3

TELEMARKETING
BASICS

Each time you answer your business phone or place a business call, you are marketing your company. Each phase of company growth is measured through telephone communication. Each time you solicit a customer, satisfy a customer or save a customer, you build your business and your telephone skills. You are a telemarketer. Each of your customers is a buyer.

Telemarketing is one of the fastest growing industries in business today...expanding at a projected 30 percent each year. Telemarketing has come a long, long way from the high-pressure, "boiler room" approach of years ago. Telemarketing today combines modern technology with a planned and managed system to sell and service virtually millions of customers and a diverse group of products and services. It is an accepted way of selling wholesale and retail products, and it is responsible for marketing everything from 50-cent magazines to heavy construction equipment costing hundreds of thousands of dollars. It has grown from approximately 170,000 businesses in 1987 to a projected 500,000 businesses in the 1990s. Whether the objective is to have a toll-free line to receive incoming orders or an outbound calling program that sells sophisticated products, telemarketing involves the same process.

What's in It for You?

With increased business costs, telemarketing has emerged as one of the most cost-effective ways of doing business. Most studies show that the average on-site sales call costs more than $200 to make. In contrast, an average telemarketing call costs around $20. Obviously you can make a lot of telemarketing calls for the price of one face-to-face contact. More and more businesses are turning to telemarketing not only to control costs but to increase sales. What does this mean to you? Opportunity. You're in an industry that's growing quickly, seeking competent people and offering career opportunities virtually everywhere.

What Does It Include?

Simply, telemarketing is doing business by telephone. As simple as this sounds, it touches virtually every aspect of business. It includes both incoming and outgoing calls, allowing customers to reach you when they want and making it possible for you to reach them with special opportunities. It's much more than just a boon to the sales department, though. Trucking firms schedule drivers, pickups and deliveries. Companies keep control of their accounts-receivable inventory and manufacturing through telemarketing. Customers are advised on questions and concerns they have. Remember the Tylenol tragedy? An 800 "hot line" was established to advise and counsel concerned customers. That, too, was a form of telemarketing. The list is endless. Virtually anything that was done face-to-face can now be done using a telemarketing application.

The Five Points of a Star

Those bright, shining stars that signify success and fame have five points. Likewise, your success and fame in telemarketing depend on how well you execute five key points of the telemarketing star. These five key areas are planning, listening, presenting, handling objections and closing. Let's take a look at each one.

1. **Planning** accomplishes three key objectives in telemarketing:

   - It allows you to be thorough and include all points necessary to make a good presentation — benefits, customer information, possible objections and closing the call.
   - Because you are prepared, you feel more confident. This confidence is passed on through your voice. Subtle but different inflections and tones send out the message of "confidence."
   - Because you are more confident, the person you're speaking to notices it automatically. He or she believes your presentation more and is more likely to buy your product or service.

2. **Listening** builds that unspoken bond between you and your customer. We've all been around a person who talked constantly and never listened. Generally, we can't wait to get away. If you do this with your customers, they will react the same way. It's also very important to put some "body language" into a phone conversation, such as saying "uh-huh," or "I see." Listening to customers' needs, both real and imagined, as well as communicating understanding and reinforcement are musts for the successful telemarketer.

3. **Presenting** needs to satisfy your customer in several ways. You must be able to present your product or service in terms

of how it will best help your customers. That's what they're interested in. Equally important, you have the chance to confirm that your customer information is correct, which helps prevent disasters such as sending them the wrong products, or billing them at the wrong address. Finally, successful presenting allows you to build a justifiable business case for your customer. Although we make many decisions emotionally, our customers have to know (and be shown) how your product or service will help their business in terms of dollars and cents.

4. **Handling Objections** is part of any sales process. There are many ways that objections are phrased, yet they all boil down to a few key types. By doing some preparation ahead of time, you will be better equipped to handle those objections calmly and effectively — something that often separates successes from failures. Understanding that objections are not personal attacks allows you to preserve your positive attitude, which is critical to your success. After all, if your customers have objections, that proves they're listening to you. Right?

5. **Closing** is the fifth point of the telemarketing star and one of the areas most neglected in sales. An effective telemarketing presentation must have three to five places where the salesperson can attempt to close. Even if your customer says "no," you can get more information to close later. Also important is the ability to recognize signs from customers that tell you they're ready to close. To succeed, you need to be able to identify opportunities, have a planned close and then ask when the opportunity arises.

Putting these five points together forms the core of a successful telemarketing presentation. You will probably be better at some of these than others, and that's normal. Become proficient in all of them, and you're on your way to breaking sales records, meeting customer needs and building your company image.

Planning for Success

Begin your telemarketing proficiency by planning for success. When people fail at many different things, "They always have an excuse." When they succeed at a few, "They always have a plan."

It has been said that one minute of planning saves three minutes of execution. It certainly creates more sales. Without a plan, you're not sure what you're trying to do, how you are going to do it or what options you have. What's worse is that's the way you sound to your customer — confused. Few sales are made this way. By planning your call, you not only feel more confident in your presentation, but you sound more confident. Before you pick up the phone, you need to prepare by getting background information on your customer and his or her business, doing some self-evaluation and finally planning your call.

Do Your Background Work

One of the most crucial elements of planning is gathering information. This includes several steps.

1. **Learn About Your Customer.**
   The more you know about your customers, the more personalized your approach can be to their businesses. This alone separates you from most of your competition. It allows you to be a consultant instead of "just" a salesperson.

   There are several helpful resources for developing background information on your customers, including:
   - Past account files
   - Other sales representatives
   - Industry publications
   - Business sections of newspapers
   - Stock prices
   - Competitors
   - Use of your product or service

2. **Learn About Their Industry.**
What departments in this industry does your product or service particularly help? For example, does it improve shipping? In what other way can you help this industry?

What industry needs can you uncover? Are there particular regulatory aids or hindrances in their industries (Occupational Safety and Health Administration, Utility Commissions, etc.) that you can offset? Do they give you new opportunities?

3. **Learn About Yourself.**
Identify and conquer the five fears associated with selling.

- **Fear of Rejection:** This means you take criticism as a personal attack, even though the criticism was directed only at your product or presentation. Solution: It's important to realize that "no" is nothing more than that. Salespeople know that they take many "nos" before they get a "yes."

- **Loss of Self-Esteem:** This is a form of self-rejection. "It's me, it's my fault, if only I could be like...." Solution: Know your product, your plan and how to help your customer. This prepares you to answer questions and objections without feeling inferior.

- **Fear of Failure:** We become afraid of trying something for fear of failing. The real or perceived negative effects of failure become too great to manage. Our society has forced us to operate on an "all or nothing," "win or lose," "success or failure" mentality. The reality is, however, that many small rejections or failures are part of the larger picture of success. Professional baseball players are paid millions of dollars per year. Yet the reality is that they generally fail more than 60 percent of the time when they bat.

The game of sales is very similar. Always remember: Sales is a numbers game, and "nos" are part of the path to "yes." Solution: Relive your past successes to fight this fear.

- **Fear of Success:** Some people have been programmed or they program themselves to avoid success. They see themselves as failures, and that becomes their reality. When they start to succeed at something, they have to find a way to fail. Deliberately making critical mistakes or failing to even try (not making a call, for example) may be symptoms of this fear. Solution: Surround yourself with positives about yourself. It's a reprogramming process that can take a long time, and professional help may be necessary. Remember, you have a right to be successful and are probably better than you think. Start reprogramming yourself.

- **Fear of the Unknown:** This is a fear present in almost every person at least to some degree. We all have concerns about the unknown. *What we really fear is not what's unfamiliar, but our inability to control a strange situation.* Solution: Constantly remind yourself that every day produces unknowns, and they aren't fatal. Also, reinforce all the positives in your life by telling yourself that they were unknowns once, too.

Some or all of these fears restrict us at one time or another. You must remember, though, that these have been allowed to grow in your subconscious since your childhood. It takes time and effort to fight them. Once these fears are managed, however, "the sky is the limit." So look at fear in the following way:

Fear

Fear — that intangible, strangling feeling that chokes success and steals our accomplishments before they occur. Nowhere is it more common and better disguised than in the simple act of talking to a customer. We all believe, at one time or another, that a horrible fate lurks at the other end of the telephone line. Why do we torture ourselves?

A unique definition of fear by an unknown author helps put this in perspective. **FEAR = F**antasized **E**vents **A**ppearing **R**eal. No person has ever had his or her birthday taken away or been physically damaged just because a customer said "no." People have, however, been damaged in their supervisors' eyes for not meeting reachable objectives. In many cases, it has boiled down to fear of an imaginary fate being *worse than the reality* of failing at a job they were capable of doing.

Some experts claim that our subconscious mind contains 85 percent of our mental ability, compared with 15 percent for our conscious part. If this is so, and repetition is a proven form of teaching, perhaps we can reverse or temper this curse. We succeed far more times each day than we fail. Our only fault is not admitting it to ourselves. Count all your successes. Soon fear will shrink to its proper size and meaning, which is nothing more than subconscious fantasies testing your proven abilities to succeed.

Plan Your Call

After evaluating yourself and doing your homework on your customer and/or industry, you need to plan the ideal call. What steps are necessary? These are the steps you need to take to plan effective calls:

1. **Set Your Objective.**
   What are you trying to do in this call? Sell a new product? Answer a question? Make an appointment or qualify a prospect? You set your goal. You have to have a target before you can hit it.

2. **Plan Your Introduction.**
   Your first impression is your best, so make sure it counts.
   Steps to a successful introduction include:

   - **Your name**
   - **Your company's name**
   - **Personalizing your introduction to the customer.** Be positive and friendly, but react according to your customer's style. If he or she wants to chat a little first, follow that lead.
   - **Making sure you're talking to decision-makers.** Does this person have the authority to purchase your product or service?
   - **Expressing a willingness to help,** if the situation calls for it. Example: Your customer may need help with a problem. By offering to help, you position yourself as a team player.
   - **Developing an interest-creating remark.** This remark ought to answer the question: Why should I listen to you? Example: "I'm calling to discuss ways of increasing your company's sales by 10 percent or more."

3. **Manage Screeners.**
   They may be hesitant about letting you talk to the person in charge. Remember, they handle hundreds of business representatives every day. Here are several hints that can help you deal with a screening assistant or secretary.

   - **Ask for their help.** You're offering a potential benefit to this company. Ask them to help you identify the person you need to talk to. Not knowing whom to talk to is no sin. Besides, it's very difficult for them to say "no" when someone is asking for their help. Example: "Could you help me? I'm new to this account, and I'm not sure who is in charge of purchasing maintenance supplies. Who would that be?"

- **Be direct.** You have many customers, and wasting their time is as bad as wasting yours. No one is fooled when you try to be cute by not indicating why you are calling.

- **Use third-party references** if applicable. A familiar name gives credibility to a stranger. Use one whenever you can.

- **Follow up on correspondence.** Sometimes a person will pay attention to a piece of mail and be much more receptive to a follow-up call. A letter can break the ice and also help you get past screeners.

- **Returning customer calls.** If you have missed a call-back, make sure the assistant or secretary knows you're returning the customer's call. It carries more credibility.

- **Call after office hours.** Sometimes a screener will be particularly difficult to deal with. If you feel you have hit a dead end, call before or after normal hours or during lunch. The boss often answers his or her own phone then.

4. **Develop Probing Questions.**
   You need to make sure you're putting the right solution with the right problem, so find out as much as you can about your customers and their needs. The easiest way is to ask questions. For probing purposes, there are two types of questions:

   - **Closed-ended questions** are generally used to confirm information. (Is your address...?)
   - **Open-ended questions** are designed to get the customer to respond. These generally can't be answered in one or two words. This type of

question provides you with most information from your customer.

Here are some samples of both open-ended and closed-ended questions:

Open-ended questions:

1. I'm curious about your inventory control, could you explain...?
2. That's interesting.... (Although this isn't a question, it often encourages your customer to keep talking.)
3. Please help me understand how you....
4. How do you feel about handling that new territory?
5. What are your thoughts regarding your maintenance costs...?
6. May I ask your reasons?

Closed-ended questions:

1. Are you interested in this particular feature or benefit?
2. Now that makes sense, doesn't it?
3. Does that seem reasonable to you?
4. That would be valuable to you, wouldn't it?
5. Am I correct in thinking...?
6. Would you agree...?
7. How does that sound/compare...?

5. **Distinguish Benefits From Features.**
All too often, a salesperson pays more attention to the features than the benefits. However, the customer buys because of the benefits to his or her business. Here's the difference:

- **Feature:** A characteristic of a product, program or service
- **Benefit:** The value received in terms of dollars saved, dollars earned, self-enhancement, time saved or elimination of fear

Hint: The easiest way to explain a benefit is to describe the feature and how it will help the customer. Example: This piece of equipment weighs only 10 pounds (feature), so that you can carry it with no problem (benefit).

Every benefit ultimately does one of three things for your customer:

1. It increases sales.
2. It decreases costs.
3. It increases profits.

6. **Plan for Objections.**
   Objections are as big a part of selling as closes are. Studies show that the average sale presentation will contain at least five customer objections. This means that you will have to prepare yourself both intellectually and emotionally for these objections.

To prepare, write down the 10 to 12 most commonly heard objections to your product or service. Once you have this list, write out an answer for each of these objections. Make sure your answers aren't argumentative. Ensure that you end each answer with the benefit your product provides. Types of objections and formats for answers appear later. It's critical to have quick, but believable, answers ready. This increases your credibility and confidence.

Preparing yourself emotionally is as important as learning to respond to objections. Be aware of two key facts associated with telemarketing:

- The average close ratio in telemarketing is about 10 percent. That means nine out of 10 people will say no. Acceptance of this fact will prevent it from chipping away at your confidence or ability to succeed.

- Objections are generally not personal attacks aimed at you. Don't take them personally. Realize what they are: subconscious requests for more information.

By taking the time to prepare yourself for specific objections and by preparing yourself mentally for the "real world" part of selling, you make yourself much stronger and able to cope much better, too.

7. **Prepare Sample Closes.**
   Closes, like objections, are inevitable parts of selling. With many salespeople, the **FEAR** of rejection stops them from reaching that point of asking for a yes or no. Not asking for the sale is one of the most common and easily corrected parts of selling. Plan at least three (and preferably five) points in your presentation that would be good times to ask for the order. Every time your customers say "no," they are forced to give you a reason. This allows you to educate them a little more on your product and further weakens their resistance.

   Use the same procedure you used for objections — write out several closes using different benefits. Some sample closes follow later in this handbook. Your customers expect you to ask for the sale, and they will give you signs that they're ready. These signals will be discussed later in greater detail. Be aware of closing signals and **ASK**. Remember, they will buy only if they can benefit by increased profits or decreased expenses. You're helping their businesses by providing them with opportunities and solutions: your products and services.

4

EFFECTIVE LISTENING TECHNIQUES

Listening is a skill most people take for granted. Most of us assume, incorrectly, that because we hear someone say something we are listening. We usually listen at 25 percent capacity or less.

Good listening skills are crucial to having good telephone skills and sales. Because you cannot see the person you speak to, there are no physical cues or clues, such as body language and eye contact, to help you focus your attention and listen effectively. You must rely solely on your ears to gather information.

Good telephone skills begin with listening, but listening involves a great deal more than just hearing. It involves the following traits:

- Empathy
- Evaluation
- Understanding
- Assimilating
- Giving feedback

An old saying states, "There are those who listen and those who wait to talk." Those who listen assimilate and think about what is said. Those who wait to talk are too busy planning what they are going to say to be paying close attention to the speaker.

If you are in the latter category, don't worry. Anyone can learn to be a good listener. It's a skill that takes practice and discipline, like playing the piano, ice skating or playing chess. Even good listeners constantly polish their skills. We all can stand to increase our listening capacity.

Listening is particularly important to those who rely on the telephone to communicate with customers because there are no visual clues to affirm or negate information. The successful telemarketer knows it is impossible to succeed in sales without good listening and communicating skills. For example, if someone tells you over the phone that "the idea is great," you can't see whether he or she says it with a genuinely enthusiastic expression or with a smirk. Since the phone takes away a key communication tool (your eyes), you have to replace it with verbal substitutes. You have to make sure you really understand what your customer is saying. Remember these important facts when you are communicating:

- Most decisions are made using emotions rather than logic.
- People's perceptions are real to them.
- The more you get someone to talk, the smarter *you* appear to them.
- Listening and communicating skills have to be practiced.

Psychologist Ray Birdwhistle notes that up to 93 percent of our communication is non-verbal. Unless you become an expert listener, you could be missing valuable information.

What are the key elements of good listening? We'll discuss them; but first, let's look at some common pitfalls that prevent people from listening well. See if you experience any of these when you listen:

- Being impatient.
- Allowing mental distractions.
- Doing two things at once.
- Making assumptions about what the speaker says or will say.

What Makes a Good Listener?

Patience
People who don't listen but wait to talk are impatient. They are more concerned with what they have to say than having a conversation. Developing patience when you listen is a valuable investment. If you patiently wait and let people talk, you'll be amazed at what they tell you. In many cases you'll learn much more than if you try to persuade them to give you information. Most good salespeople know that you sell more by listening than by talking.

Concentration
Mental distractions are a common pitfall to effective listening. People who allow distractions to interfere with their listening have too many things on their minds. They may think about a report they have to do, a deadline that's approaching, family problems, or they may merely daydream. In any event, they fail to concentrate on what the person who is speaking says.

Some people think they can listen effectively and think about something else at the same time. While they may be able to repeat words that were said, most of the time they can't recall the subtleties of the conversation.

More importantly, it is virtually impossible to hide your distraction from someone who wants your attention.

Focus

It is tempting to do two things at once when you talk on the telephone. Some people try to listen while paying bills, going through the mail, or even worse, while listening to someone in their office talk.

Like mental distractions, physical distractions make it almost impossible to hear the innuendo in a conversation or provide adequate feedback. You will have shorter and more productive telephone conversations if you focus on doing just one thing — listening.

Open-mindedness

Another pitfall is making assumptions about what you think someone is going to say. Once you make assumptions, you have a separate mental conversation where you debate those assumptions. This involves a great deal of your attention and energy that should be devoted to listening.

Don't make assumptions. Start a conversation with an open mind. Let the other party tell you what's on his or her mind.

Listening Blocks

There are certain attitudes and situations that restrict our ability to listen effectively. Sometimes they are physical, like loud background noises, and sometimes they are mental. Prejudice is an example of a mental listening block. Regardless of which type of block you experience, the effect is the same. Listening blocks disrupt your ability to concentrate and absorb every drop of information your customer is giving you — information that might lead to a sale. Here are the most common listening blocks:

1. **Environmental/Physical**

    You may not be aware of how much background noise interferes with either your ability to listen or communicate. Be aware of background noises that may be drowning out your voice or putting your customer in second place.

2. **Personal Biases**
You may harbor unknown dislikes or attitudes about certain people. These often override attempts at listening and close you off emotionally. Fight the urge and stay objective.

3. **Fatigue**
It is very possible, particularly at the end of a long, hard day, to be so tired that you are just "going through the motions."

Techniques to Overcome Listening Blocks

1. **Limit Your Own Talking.**
You can't talk and listen at the same time.

2. **Think Like the Customer.**
His or her problems and needs are important, and you'll understand them better if you keep the customer's point of view in mind.

3. **Ask Questions.**
If you don't understand something, clear it up now before it embarrasses you.

4. **Be Patient.**
A pause, even a long pause, doesn't always mean the customer is finished.

5. **Concentrate.**
Focus on what your customer is saying. Practice shutting out distractions.

6. **Listen for People's Ideas, Not Just to Their Words.**
People may speak differently than you, but don't be thrown off course. Listen not only to the words, but also for emphasis, the context of what they are saying and the overall direction of the conversation.

7. **Use Interjections.**
An occasional "yes," "I see," "Oh, really," serves the same purpose as eye contact and head nods in a conversation — they let the customer know you are listening to him or her.

8. **Turn off Your Own Worries.**
Don't be distracted by last night's argument with your spouse or the unpaid bills. Practice closing your mind to anything not connected to your customer.

9. **Don't Argue Mentally.**
You may not agree with what your customer is saying, but keep an open mind. You may uncover a new opportunity or even learn something new!

10. **Don't Jump to Conclusions.**
Much like impulsively saying something that damages your image, don't damage your opportunities by making assumptions before you have heard everything your customer has to say. Hear him or her out!

11. **Listen for Overtones.**
The way customers say things is often more important than what they say. Listen for emotions such as sarcasm, irritation or relief in their voices.

12. **Practice Listening.**
Practice with friends, family and associates. You become professional through practice.

What Is Your Listening Speed?

Many people are aware of how fast or slowly they speak, but few ever think about how fast they listen. One of the primary reasons our minds tend to wander during a conversation is because we listen much faster than most people speak.

For instance, most Americans speak at the rate of 180 words per minute. However, because our minds work much more quickly, we can listen at a rate of *600 words per minute!* It's easy to understand why our minds get bored waiting for a speaker to make a point.

You can keep your mind focused on the speaker several ways:

- **Take Notes.**
  As a person speaks, take notes. This is easy to do when you are on the telephone because you don't have to maintain eye contact with the speaker. Taking notes necessitates a slower listening speed and allows you to concentrate on what the speaker says.

- **Ask Questions.**
  Asking questions is an effective technique for slowing your listening speed. When combined with taking notes, it allows you to ask relevant questions, which greatly enhance your ability to communicate effectively.

- **Provide Continual Feedback.**
  When you decide it is important to participate in the conversation, it becomes essential to pay close attention to what is being said. Feedback does not include responses such as "I understand," "That's interesting," "Oh," or assorted other affirmative grunts. It means summarizing or paraphrasing key points the speaker makes with responses such as "If I understand you correctly, then the report has the following implications...." Taking notes throughout the conversation makes feedback easy.

By slowing your listening and using the techniques we've outlined, you can create a powerful image as an interested, concerned, intelligent listener.

Techniques to Good Listening Feedback

As you are beginning to see, listening is only part of the communication process. Customers can't see you, but they need the reinforcement and feedback that keep them talking. This is where good listening feedback comes in. Knowing how to reassure, rephrase and question keeps customers relaxed and the contact positive, giving you a head start toward customer satisfaction.

Here are some techniques to provide feedback:

1. **Reassurances**

   This is a form of feedback directed at the emotional side of your customer. All people have hopes, fears, greeds and emotional needs that must be recognized and resolved, if possible. There are several ways to do this:

   - Sounds of encouragement (Examples: "Uh huh," "I see," "Oh.")
   - Words of recognition ("I understand how you feel.")
   - Use silence. Don't interrupt if they're upset or "blowing up." Let them get rid of their anger or frustration first.

   One word of caution: don't overuse these expressions. Using them three or four times in a conversation is plenty.

2. **Restating**
By summarizing a customer's major points or paraphrasing in your own words, you accomplish two things:

- You confirm the information is correct.
- You get the customer to agree with you. ("That's right.") By getting your customer to agree with you, you subconsciously break barriers, thus improving your chances for a sale.

3. **Questioning**
This is where you really put your communication skills to use. For various reasons, the more your customer talks, the smarter he or she thinks you are. You need to plan your questioning to use proven techniques:

- We discussed questions using the open-ended style. Some words that you can begin your questions with are who, what, where, when, why and how.
- Use confirming questions. As discussed earlier, these confirm ordinary information. However, they can also be used to get hesitant customers talking. Many times they'll say "yes" or "no" a few times and relax.

Communicating Tips

How you sound on the telephone can have a significant impact on the perceptions the listener forms about you and what you are selling. Keep the following points in mind:

1. **Volume**
Your volume should be the same as if you were talking to someone across the table (who is three to five feet away).

2. Rate

Rate of speech varies depending on what part of the country you're from, but you should average 180 words per minute. If you are too slow, customers get bored. If you are too fast, they can't understand and get frustrated. Practice on the following statement — it should take about 60 seconds.

180-Word Statement

Most experts agree that the ideal rate of speech is between 180 to 200 words per minute. At this rate, people who are listening to you will be able to hear and understand what you are saying. In the United States there are different patterns of speech that are the product of geographic areas. In the northeast part of the country, people tend to speak faster than others, while people from the South speak slower than the ideal rate. However, people in the Midwest tend to speak at the 180-word rate. Use the second hand of a clock to do this. If you read this statement in less than a minute, you are speaking too fast and should make an effort to slow down. If you read this statement in more than a minute, you are speaking too slowly and should try to speak faster when talking on the phone.

3. Tone/Pitch

Although very difficult to determine, tone can be a real asset or liability. If you say "uh-hum" in your regular volume, that will be close to the tone and pitch you should use. Have an honest friend give you feedback on your tone.

4. Breathing

Because your breathing should come from your torso, you should see your stomach rise and fall as you breathe. This type of breathing allows you to control your tone better and gives more "power" to your voice.

5. Articulation

There are several areas included here, all dealing with speech:

- **Posture:** Sit on the front half of your chair. This forces you to sit up straight and allows your voice to have more power and clarity.
- **Obstacles:** Cigarettes, gum and candy should never compete with your teeth and tongue. Avoid putting things in your mouth when you're on the phone.
- **Slang:** Although it's an accepted form of communication, your customer may not know your local slang. It creates confusion and frustration, so stay away from it.
- **Technical Terms/Jargon:** For many of us, it's very easy to get excited about new developments in our products and services. Remember though, the customer only cares what benefit they provide. Don't use technical terms unless they help explain a benefit.

6. Attitudes

Your attitude is the first thing your customer will notice. It can make you or break you. You may not impress everyone, but you'll offend the fewest possible customers if you act friendly, helpful and positive.

7. Answering Promptly

Answer within three rings, if possible.

8. Names

Listen to how your customers use your name and how they introduce themselves. If they're comfortable with first names, go with them. If they're more formal and use Mr. and Ms., you do the same. Using their names three times in a conversation is about normal.

9. **Using a Recorder**
There's no better way of improving yourself than hearing and critiquing the way you speak. Don't get discouraged, though. Practice pays huge dividends.

Evaluate Your Listening Skills

Evaluate your listening skills and determine where you may need improvement by answering the following questions:

1. Do I judge from the speaker's tone of voice and delivery whether what he or she says is worthwhile?
2. Do I listen for ideas, underlying feelings and subtle messages?
3. Do I know my biases and put them in perspective?
4. Does my mind wander when I listen to someone talk?
5. Do I interrupt when someone makes an incorrect statement?
6. Do I give good feedback?
7. Do I evaluate the logic and credibility of what I hear?
8. Do I have to have the last word?
9. Do I focus the conversation on myself or the other party?
10. Do I effectively control the length of the conversation? Do I get frustrated and impatient if it drags on?

The answers to these questions will help you develop a strategy for improving your listening skills. As part of this strategy you can incorporate the following hints from experienced telephone professionals:

- Avoid chatter or conversation with needless comments such as "you know," "I mean," and "as a matter of fact." These make you sound inarticulate.
- Avoid digressions or changes in the subject if the conversation is going well.
- Avoid focusing the conversation on yourself or offering too

much personal information. Ask others about themselves and their interests.

- Be relevant. Pay close attention to the points made by the other party. React to those points, not something unrelated.
- Address the other party by name, especially if you feel you are not being listened to or want to make an important point. People tend to pay closer attention when their names are used.

Self-Inventory

After learning about different strategies and techniques for good listening and communicating, you have the tools to become a much more effective communicator. Here are lists of effective and ineffective techniques. Use these lists as reminders.

Effective Telephone Techniques

1. Smile.
2. Speak clearly and concisely.
3. Be enthusiastic.
4. Lower your voice pitch.
5. Talk in positives.
6. Be prepared for objections.
7. Talk directly into the mouthpiece.
8. Consider your customer's personality.
9. Speak in terms of benefits.
10. Discuss rather than tell.
11. Always thank the listener for his time.
12. Follow up if necessary.

Ineffective Telephone Techniques

1. Frowning
2. Muttering
3. Sounding tired
4. Speaking in a monotone
5. Being negative
6. Being overconfident
7. Holding the telephone under your chin
8. Rambling
9. Making accusatory remarks
10. Arguing
11. Hanging up abruptly
12. Forgetting to thank the listener
13. Trying to talk and do something else at the same time

TWELVE COMMON CUSTOMER STYLES

You are in business to satisfy the customer and to represent your company. The best way to do both simultaneously is to identify your customer's style. By doing so, you can more quickly address the customer's needs or suggest solutions to the customer's problems. The customer's buying style reflects his or her personality and communication style. Knowing the twelve most common styles will provide you with the insight you need to do your job better and more easily.

Buying Styles

An excellent means of analyzing your customer is to determine what type of buyer the person is. There are many styles of people and many styles of buyers. Here are the most common:

1. **The Know-It-All Buyer**
   This person may be an "expert buyer," whatever that means.

Here are some characteristics:

- Knows everything about you and your product or service
- Will swamp you with questions
- May stop you in the middle of your presentation
- Will appear to pay very little attention to what you say
- Will probably stop your phone conversation suddenly

Here are some suggestions on how to impress the know-it-all buyer:

- Arouse his or her curiosity. Build suspense for your product.
- Listen very carefully to what he or she says and how. The buyer will give you facts you can agree with to position yourself better.
- Play to the ego. Use statements that build ego. For example: "With your expertise in this field, I know others follow your lead."

2. **The Open-Minded Buyer**

Although this person sounds like the buyer everyone wants to talk with, he or she isn't that easy to sell. Many inexperienced telemarketers mistake open-mindedness for empty-mindedness. This buyer is receptive to new products, applications and concepts, but is interested from a business standpoint.

An open-minded buyer will do some of these things:

- Will be interested in your presentation if it sounds appealing
- Will be friendly and polite
- Will ask questions about your product because

he or she is a good listener
- Will make honest objections
- Will buy from you if you earn the sale

There are several things you can do to improve your chances with these buyers:

- Answer all questions politely.
- Be friendly with them.
- Don't talk down to them. They will probably understand everything you say. If they don't, they'll ask.

3. **The Lonesome Buyer**

Sometimes this person can be mistaken for the open-minded buyer. He or she will accept your call, sound very friendly and like to hear about your product, but will end up wasting your time. This buyer rarely buys anything.

Here are some of the lonesome buyer's characteristics:

- Will be polite and friendly like an open-minded buyer
- Will encourage you to continue with your presentation and be enthusiastic
- Will be a good listener and is probably smiling during your presentation
- Will agree with all the benefits you mention
- Is rarely specific about time; generally doesn't make appointments and won't care if you run a little longer in your presentation

Here are some suggestions on how to qualify and manage these buyers:

- Be specific about their interests and needs. This is for your protection. You may waste much of your valuable telephone selling time on an unqualified buyer.

- If a call-back is necessary, make sure you pin someone down for a specific time with a specific agenda.
- Prolong the telephone conversation with your buyer until you can determine commitments to specifics: needs, qualifications and objections.
- If you determine that you do have a lonesome buyer, don't waste any more time than necessary. Be friendly and polite, but end your telephone call as quickly as you can. Agree to stay in touch and give him or her time to think about it, but move on.

4. **The Uncertain Buyer**

As the title implies, these buyers don't make strong decisions. In fact, they have trouble making any decision. Many times, you have to make the decision for them.

Here are some of the uncertain buyer's characteristics:

- Will not be able to make a decision; can't deal with issues in a straightforward manner, and would not be able to maintain eye contact if seen in person
- Will stall or procrastinate and, even on the phone, will not commit to things
- Always needs to talk to somebody else before making a decision; therefore removes himself or herself from the responsible position

Here's how to control these buyers and succeed:

- Don't give them too many options or ideas. Two is the best number.
- Don't allow them to control time. You set the

time and length of your call. If a call-back is
necessary, give them two choices when you'll call
back.

- Offer positive, objective answers to subjective
  objections. Don't let their vague objections win.
- If they make an objection, agree with them.
  Then switch to a positive benefit for your product.
  The important point here is not to let their
  objection sway you.
- Be definite and positive in your tone and manner.
  This confidence will come over well on the phone.
- If they want to talk to someone else, encourage
  them to do so. Then suggest a conference call,
  offer to answer any implementation or technical
  questions they have and arrange to call back at
  a specific time.

This type of buyer is best controlled by being firm and
straightforward. These buyers don't like conflict and confrontation. Don't threaten them but be strong — it will work.

5. **The Timid Buyer**
   This type of buyer can be trouble for two reasons. First, this
   person has a very difficult time making a decision, particularly
   over the phone. Second, this person often is hostile toward
   salespeople and sometimes will cancel the sale after you
   have hung up.

Here are some timid buyers' characteristics:

- Express hostility toward you, and you may detect
  fear in their voices also
- State objections mildly
- Switch from one decision to another
- Agree with you on everything — and too easily
- Forget parts of past contracts that involved key
  benefits of your presentation

These are some suggestions to help you deal with timid buyers:

- Keep buyers feeling as comfortable as you can. Don't act in a threatening manner. Be as friendly and reassuring as possible.
- Empathize with buyers. Try to understand their feelings, particularly objections.
- Make sure you give your customer all the benefits and pluses of your product.
- Keep the confidence in your voice. This decisiveness reassures customers more than almost anything. Be friendly, positive and confident. It will work.

6. The Hard-Headed Buyer

Once you have gained this customer's confidence; he is extremely loyal. Hard-headed buyers have certain similarities:

- They're protective of their time. They don't agree to a phone presentation easily.
- They're very blunt. When they object, they're almost rude.
- They're stubborn. They cling to their way of thinking to a fault.
- They're control-oriented. They intimidate either with questions or with statements.

To win this buyer you should do several things to highlight the benefits of your product or service and yourself:

- Don't disagree with these customers. By agreeing with them, you prevent them from finding an issue they can use to drive between them and you.
- Show them as much respect as you can. Build their egos whenever possible.

- Stress a teamwork strategy. Convince them that you're calling to help them.
- Play to their curious side. They have a lot of curiosity. Use this to increase their interest in your call.

7. **The Dissatisfied Buyer**

This is the person who always has something negative to say. It may be about the product, service, company or almost anything. Whoever happens to call this person gets the bulk of his or her negativism. Just remember it's nothing personal.

Here are some of the dissatisfied buyer's characteristics:

- Will express frustration and blame someone or something
- Will start complaining when you first call and will want your understanding
- Won't pay much, if any, attention to what you have to say

There are several things you can do to handle these buyers:

- Accept the blame right away so you diffuse their major objection up front. They can't disagree or criticize if you agree with them.
- Agree that their complaints are worthwhile and valid.
- Be sympathetic with their emotions. For example, "I don't blame you for complaining. If I got a shipment delivered two weeks late, I'd be mad, too."
- Find a way to gain their agreement on something to break the negative trend. Then you can build more points of agreement as you continue your phone call.

- Act quickly and decisively to correct their problems.
- Don't take their complaints to heart.

8. The Expressive Buyer

This is the buyer who may intimidate you in the first few seconds of your telephone call. There is a lot of emotion in this facade, but don't let it sway you.

Here are some points to remember about expressive buyers:

- They are emotional and can be influenced by emotional presentations.
- They can appear to be very self-centered and talk about themselves.
- They may show irritation that you called, as though you were interrupting something very important. They will also have a quick and probably emotional objection to your call.
- They won't appear to pay any attention to your sales presentation. You may encounter interruptions from them as they talk to other people in their offices.
- Their only interest may be "what's in it for me."

To be successful with expressive buyers, there are several things you need to do:

- Refer to what they will gain from this purchase.
- Knowing that they can be self-centered, play to their ego and/or pride.
- Use testimonials and references. These public approvals appeal to them and improve your chances of selling to them.
- Make them curious from your opening statement. If they hear that they will gain a benefit, they'll be much more likely to listen.

9. The Analytical Buyer
This person is a curious information-gatherer who will ask more questions than any other buyer.

Here are some ways you can identify these buyers:

- They want more information. They may ask for it over the phone, or they may ask that you mail it to them.
- "How" is a commonly used word for this buyer. "How does it work?" "How do you service it?" "How do you deliver?"
- They also need to have more information on you and your company. "How big are you?" "What customers do you deal with?" "How much experience do you have?"

Their logic, curiosity and thorough approach are their strengths. Appeal to these qualities when you are on the phone with them:

- Show them how your product will help them. Get their interest as quickly as you can.
- Don't "dump" all your benefits on them at once. Give them the chance to digest this information and ask for more.
- Be reasonable with these people. They thrive on logic and reason, so appeal to theirs.

10. The Bargain Buyer
These buyers come across as being too poor to buy anything, but don't believe them. They just negotiate from a "poor me, how good a price can I get?" stance.

Here are some characteristics of bargain buyers:

- "How much is it?" is generally asked early in the telephone call. If cost isn't brought up quickly, how much they can save will be.
- They may say your product or service is priced too high or that they don't have the money for it in the budget.
- They might "sing the blues" or tell you how bad things are right now.
- Rarely will they ask about issues such as warranty, disability service, etc.

11. The Intimidating Buyer

These buyers more than any others use a facade or false front. Their first defense is their strongest and possibly only defense. Here are some ways you can recognize them:

- They will try to intimidate you or put you on the defensive.
- They will try to control the telephone conversation. They may do this by being very loud or abrupt, even rude. They may also appear to get angry very easily.
- They will not initially allow you any time or be courteous.

However, there are ways of successfully dealing with these buyers:

- Don't apologize for calling or take the blame for anything.
- Be courteous and friendly, but don't give in to their bullying tactics. Show your strength of will and character.
- Play to their egos and agree with them when it doesn't compromise you or your position.

- Be reasonable with them. Keep their needs and desires in mind. Appeal to their reason and logic.

These buyers will come around, but they have to see that you aren't a threat to them and that you won't be intimidated by their actions.

12. **The Self-Centered Buyer**
This buyer is interested in his or her own self-determined objectives and is not interested in the give-and-take of most telemarketing presentations. Look for these characteristics to identify these buyers:

- They will talk to you in terms of themselves and their wants.
- They may refuse to talk to you at first. If they tell you why they won't talk to you, it will most likely be in a very abrupt manner.
- They won't listen to you very well. They don't care what you have to say unless it fits in with their plans.
- They won't commit to buying. They have to feel it was their decision and on their terms.

There are several hints to help you with these buyers:

- Appeal to their unique needs or wants.
- Ask them questions related to their needs, but make sure you have a purpose in mind that reinforces their objectives.
- Don't make small talk or ask trivial questions. Keep the call on track — their track.
- Don't interrupt them when they are talking.
- Stimulate their thinking about themselves and their needs as much as possible.

These 12 buying styles represent most customers. They apply to how readily a customer will buy a product, a service or an idea. Your company may provide several ways of meeting your customers' needs, and you must know the best way to present them to each customer. This knowledge saves time, frustration and money in each contact with the customer. Keep these tips handy for easy reference.

6

YOUR TELEPHONE
PRESENTATIONS

Each time you speak on the phone on behalf of your company, you make a presentation. Some presentations are more formal than others, yet all are important indicators of success. Cold calls and collection calls are especially difficult. This chapter includes techniques for telephone success.

Initiating Telephone Calls: How to Increase Your Effectiveness

Many of you rely on the telephone for your livelihood. You solve problems for customers, sell products or services and otherwise depend on successful communication by telephone.

While many of you may be comfortable receiving orders or even complaints from customers, you view initiating a call entirely differently. If you are in sales or telemarketing, many of the calls you initiate are "cold calls": calls you make to people you've never spoken with and who aren't expecting your call.

Cold calls are the most intimidating because there is a high probability that the person you call will not respond with interest or enthusiasm. The potential for rejection is high. This reality causes many people to dread picking up the phone. There are attitudes and skills you can learn, however, that will make you more comfortable and effective when you initiate any telephone call. The following list will help:

1. **Have the Right Attitude.**
   What you are doing is a job and, in many cases, the reactions of others have a lot to do with their jobs. A secretary is expected to screen his or her boss's telephone calls, and someone in purchasing is approached by dozens of salespeople each day. The people must use a filtering system to be effective in their jobs.

   Because you can't control the motivations or behavior of people, it is vital that you not take negative responses personally. See it as part of the process.

   Your attitude should be positive and confident. You need to feel good about the product or service you sell, the company you represent and yourself as a professional. You need to feel confident that you can sell a product, solve a problem or get the information you need.

   If you have this attitude, you will develop a style that is professional, persuasive and, above all, effective.

2. **Avoid Triteness.**
   Many of us begin a telephone conversation with standard phrases such as "How are you today?" This is fine for routine conversations, but if you want to make a lasting impact you must go beyond triteness to originality.

   Tape record your opening comments on the phone for one day. Do you sound like every other salesperson or telephone solicitor? If so, you will be treated as one. Be original, especially with your introduction.

WRONG: "Mrs. Derr? Hi, how are you today? My name is Karen Lee. I'm calling for Mothers Against Drunk Driving, and we'd like to know if you're interested in donating to our cause."

RIGHT: "Mrs. Derr? My name is Karen Lee. I'm helping Mothers Against Drunk Driving make the roads safer for you and your children, and we need your help."

What's the difference? The right way quickly states a benefit to listeners and then involves them by asking for their help.

WRONG: "Hello, Mr. Blake? How are you today? I'm calling for Consumer Research, and I wonder if you can answer a few questions for me. It will only take five minutes."

RIGHT: "Mr. Blake? I'm calling for Consumer Research. You are one of a select group of people chosen to participate in an important consumer-research survey. Your responses will be completely confidential. This survey takes approximately five minutes. If this isn't a convenient time, when can I call back?"

The first approach makes answering the survey sound like a time-consuming chore. If you interrupt someone, chances are the answer will be "no." The second approach makes listeners feel important because they are in a "select group," the survey is "important" and their responses will be "confidential." Also, there is a combination of respect for their time and persistence that is persuasive.

Be sure your first words engage the listener by:

- Stating a benefit
- Arousing curiosity
- Creating involvement

Trite openings lead to bored listeners who quickly reject you.

3. **Ask Assertively.**
Many people are not given respect because they don't demand it from others. Whether it's in their words or tone of voice, their approach is tentative and sometimes even apologetic rather than assertive.

> WRONG: "Could I speak with..."
> RIGHT "I need to speak with..."
>
> WRONG: "Is Mr. Brown in?"
> RIGHT: "Bill Brown, please."

In the first example, the caller asks for permission, which means whoever receives the call is in control. The right way conveys urgency and authority.

The second example implies that the caller and Mr. Brown are strangers: a red flag to anyone who screens Mr. Brown's calls. Also, asking if he's in gives Mr. Brown's secretary the option of screening the call. The right way is assertive and implies that the caller and Mr. Brown know each other. There is also the implication that Mr. Brown will speak to the caller.

Telephone professionals quickly identify callers who aren't in control. And when this happens, they begin to control the caller. You can't be in control or persuasive if you convey the message, "Well, I hope I can speak with this person, but, well...." Know who and what you want; then communicate it in an assertive and professional manner.

4. **Listen for Subtle Messages.**
Without visual cues, we have to make assumptions about the attitudes and moods of the people we want to influence over the telephone. By identifying subtle messages, you can gain valuable information about the other party's behavior and receptiveness to your call.

Two of these subtle messages are intent and tone:

- *How was the telephone answered?*
  Did the other party say, "How may I help you?" If so, you can assume whomever you are talking to has time or is willing to make time for calls.
- *What tone of voice did you hear?*
  Was the other party's tone of voice brusque? Pleasant? Open? Agitated? Don't listen entirely to the words used. Listen to the tone of voice. If you sense a less-than-open attitude, confront it directly. You can say, "Mr. Smith, is this a convenient time to talk or would you like me to call you this afternoon?" This conveys your sensitivity to time constraints and that you are cooperative.

5. **Ask Questions.**
If you haven't received any negative messages, ask a few open-ended questions. If the other party gives a relatively lengthy response, you can assume that he or she is interested in the conversation and has the time to continue it. If you run into "yes" and "no" answers, the person may be distracted or not interested in the subject. Keep probing as long as you get neutral to positive responses, or until you find a topic that involves the other party. If you run into a dead end, suggest

another time to talk or move on to the next person on your "hit" list. You won't be successful with every call, so cut your losses and search for individuals who take an active role in the conversation.

6. **Be Prepared.**
Any time you initiate a telephone call, personal or business, know what the call's purpose is and what you want to say. Especially in business situations, there is nothing worse than taking up someone's time while you organize your thoughts.

If you are in sales or telemarketing, have your presentation in writing. If you are experienced in making these calls and are thoroughly familiar with the product or service you represent, then a comprehensive written outline suffices. If you are new to either the profession or the company you represent, then prepare a script you can read until you are comfortable with what you are selling.

Part of your script or outline should include questions you can ask as well as answers to questions you anticipate. Being prepared means:

- Doing your homework
- Becoming familiar with the needs of those you plan to call
- Knowing how you or your company intends to meet those needs

If you are in customer service, this means becoming totally familiar with customer complaints, alternatives and solutions and how your company is prepared to rectify situations *before* you ever pick up the telephone. Finally, immediately state your name and the purpose of your call. Don't beat around the bush or engage in idle chitchat.

7. **Give the Listener Alternatives.**
When you initiate a telephone call, there are numerous barriers you may confront. Here are some of the most common barriers:

- Reaching someone at an inconvenient time
- Talking to people who don't think they need to talk to you
- Talking to someone who is having a bad day
- Talking to an angry customer or vendor

One of the most effective ways of dealing with these situations is to give the other party alternatives. Have these prepared and tailor them to fit each situation. Alternatives provide options and prevent the other party from responding negatively.

Here are some alternatives:

- Offering to call back at a more convenient, but specific, time
- Offering to send information to a prospective customer to review if he or she can't or won't talk to you when you call
- Offering angry customers several solutions to their problems

Making Appointments

The "cold call" is the most difficult call to make in business. The chance of rejection or hostility is high. Part of a cold call is making an appointment with someone who may be reluctant to meet with you.

Practice making appointments on safe calls that have a low chance of rejection or hostility, such as an appointment with your dentist or hair stylist. The confidence you gain on safe calls will transfer to those more difficult calls later.

Begin by giving your name, the purpose of your call, the specific service you require and two specific dates and times that are convenient for you. Once the appointment is negotiated, give your phone number where you can be reached during the day and repeat the appointment topic, date and time for verification. Say thank you, allowing the other party to hang up, and then you are done. Use this same approach for setting up your next teleconference.

Calling Times

You can leverage your appointment success by knowing when you can best reach your customer. Here are some suggestions on the best time to call different kinds of customers.

Customer	Best Calling Time
Bankers	Before 10 a.m. or after 3 p.m.
Barbers	Monday
Builders	Before 9 a.m. or after 5 p.m.
Chemists	Between 4 p.m. and 5 p.m.
Clergy	Monday, Thursday or Friday
Contractors	Before 9 a.m. or after 5 p.m.
Dentists	Before 9:30 a.m.
Executives	Between 10 a.m. and noon or between 5 p.m. and 5:30 p.m.
Farmers	Lunch time or evenings
Grocers	Between 1 p.m. and 3 p.m.
Homemakers	Between 10 a.m. and noon
Lawyers	Between 11 a.m. and 2 p.m.
Pharmacists	Between 1 p.m. and 3 p.m.
Physicians	Between 9 a.m. and 11 a.m. or after 4 p.m.
Professors/Teachers	Before 8 a.m. or after 4 p.m.
Public Accountants	Anytime *except* January through April

Publishers/Printers	After 3 p.m.
Retailers	Between 8 a.m. and 10 a.m.
Stockbrokers	Before 10 a.m. or after 3 p.m.
Wage earners (hourly)	Evenings at home before 9 p.m.

Collecting Accounts Receivable

Making cold calls and arranging appointments are only part of making your company successful. You have to make sure the product or service is delivered on time and that you receive prompt payment. If the money doesn't come in, your company has to borrow money to stay in business, thus increasing your cost of doing business. It is in your best interest to make sure payments are on time. Sometimes this involves prompting your customers who are delinquent in payments. Although this can be done by mail, it is much faster and far more effective if it's done by phone. There are certain things to consider, however, to make this effort successful.

SET OBJECTIVES
Collecting accounts receivable can be a very sensitive situation. You certainly have a right to your payment, but you don't want to alienate your customer. You have two key objectives:

1. Bring the overdue account up to current status.
2. Keep your customer satisfied with your company.

DEVELOP A COLLECTION PERSONALITY
Often it is easier to approach the difficult task of collections by adopting a "collection personality." This allows you to detach yourself emotionally and remain calm and objective. Here are the key components of this personality:

1. *Earn Respect.* Be authoritative but not confrontational. Make sure you sound confident and deal with your customer in a mature manner.
2. *Keep the Call on a Business Level.* You can and should be friendly. Don't be too familiar, though. It is a business matter and needs to be handled as such. The best approach to take is one of firm courtesy.
3. *Be Positive.* Understanding, courtesy and firm objectivity are necessary. Vulgarity, threats and humiliation have no place here. They only create ill will.
4. *Stay Flexible.* Sometimes a little compassion can make your customer feel you're really trying to help. Determine if there are legitimate reasons for the delay in payment. Work with your customer to devise a way to meet both of your needs.
5. *Be Yourself.* Don't try to be anyone but yourself. Stay calm, speak simply and don't hurry your delivery.

IDENTIFY CUSTOMER DEFENSES

No customer enjoys being told that he or she owes money and is not honoring the bargain. In addition to affecting business cash flow, it affects the customer on an emotional level. There are four negative defenses that you may encounter:

1. **Aggression**

   Your call is going to be a source of stress for your customer, who may react by criticizing or complaining about your product or service or procedures. *Don't fall into this trap.* Don't get defensive. These points aren't the issue. If the customer has a legitimate complaint, it can be dealt with separately. Don't be side-tracked. He or she bought the product or service and owes you money. Discuss when you expect payment. Then encourage the customer to get all the facts to you that pertain to the complaint by a certain date. This puts the responsibility on the customer. If he or she doesn't do this, he or she weakens the objection. If there is a legitimate problem, you have done a great service for your customer and your company.

2. **Request for Sympathy**
Regardless of what the story is, don't debate it. Be sympathetic, but remember the customer does owe you money for a product or service you already provided. If the problem honestly affects the ability to pay, you can work out a payment schedule. Be specific on terms and details.

3. **Open Defiance**
Your customer may be openly defiant. He may simply say "so?" Don't get angry. Recognize it for what it is — an attempt to knock you off target. Be persistent, and the customer may eventually tell you what the real problem is. If the customer continues to refuse, inform him or her in a calm but firm way that if the bill isn't paid by a certain date, you will submit it for collection by professionals. Always face aggression and arrogance with calm composure.

4. **Avoidance or Evasion**
Your customer may deny knowing anything about the bill. Don't try to prove a lie: it only creates animosity. Review the specifics and request immediate payment. The customer may promise to pay and fail to do so. Be aware of this tactic. Stay on him or her. More than likely, the customer is short of cash.

HAVE A CALL FORMAT

To make an effective collecting call, you must remain calm and unemotional. *You* have to be in control. To do this and be prepared properly, you need to format your call. Here is a suggested plan to follow:

1. **Identify Yourself and Your Company.**
Make sure you're talking to the person who can resolve this.

By identifying yourself, you give professionalism to your company, the purpose of your call and yourself.

2. State Your Reason for Calling.
Remember, you don't want to be clever or closed-minded to the customer's side of the story. A simple statement such as "Mr. _____, I'm calling about your bill for $2,000. It's 30 days past due." Be neither hostile nor too friendly. Just be direct, honest and firm.

3. Pause.
Don't say anything after your opening statement. A pause of six to eight seconds subconsciously puts the burden on your customer. The reply will tell you how to continue your call.

4. Fact-Find with Your Customer.
It is very important to remember that it could be a problem your company created. Listen to what your customer says to you. If it's not your company's fault, he or she will give the information necessary to establish a payment plan.

5. Transition to a Plan of Payment.
You need to move your customer into a listening mode now. Use a statement like, "I think I know a way to bring you up to current status."

6. Suggest Your Plan.
Now is when you suggest your solution to your customer. In presenting your plan, keep two things in mind:

- *It needs to be a specific payment schedule,* describing when and how it will be made current. This payment schedule needs to be understood by both parties.
- *You need to be flexible.* An alternative to your

suggestion may not be paid as quickly as yours, but it may be acceptable. Don't discount it just because it's not your idea.

7. Be Prepared to Answer Objections.

The majority of objections will be postponement-oriented. Three steps can help you handle most objections:

- *Identify exactly what your customer objects to.* Are the payments too high? Is the term too short? Once you know the exact objection, you can move to other areas.
- *Get your customer to agree to the rest of the plan.* If the payments are too high, get agreement on the amount owed, payment dates, etc. This gets the customer agreeing and makes the final discrepancy easier to resolve.
- *Reach a compromise on the disputed part.* Make sure you can explain how the customer benefits by agreeing with your compromise suggestions. Benefits such as earning early payment discounts and eliminating late charges and credit-rating risks all work here.

8. Close Your Call.

Now that you and your customer are in agreement, you need to close the call on a positive note. Include two key points in your close:

- *Summarize the agreement you've reached.* Make sure you are specific about amounts and payment dates.
- *Thank your customer.* He or she did have to work with you on this problem. Make sure you acknowledge the help. This also leaves a good impression. Remember, your customer may

have a problem now, but may be a bigger customer later. Don't risk losing your customer through a lack of courtesy.

Most overdue situations can be handled using these guidelines. However, following up is still necessary. Here are three steps to include in the follow-up:

1. **Keep Notes.**
   Make sure you do this right after the call while the details are still fresh.

2. **Update Each Customer Record.**
   In case you have to contact your customer more than once (and you may have to), this will provide an accurate history of what has occurred and been discussed. This makes you better prepared to deal with repeated problems or chronic "slow pays."

3. **Do What You Promise.**
   If you and your customer agree on a payment by the 15th of the month and it doesn't arrive, call and let your customer know. Start the process over again. If your efforts don't succeed, don't hesitate to turn the account over for collection.

TELEPHONE TIPS

There are certain things you can do to be more effective with your collection calls. For quick reference, they have been broken down into a "do" list and a "don't" list.

DO:

- Learn all you can about your customer and his or her background.
- Think positively. Have faith that things can be explained or resolved.

- Identify the person you are talking to. If this person is not the decision-maker, ask for the person who is.
- Stay calm and courteous.
- Request the full amount owed. It may be in several payments, but it needs to be in full.
- Treat your customer as you would like to be treated.

DON'T:

- Be antagonistic or sarcastic. All this does is make an uncomfortable situation worse.
- Prejudge your customer. Just because he or she owes you money doesn't mean he or she is a "deadbeat."
- Lose your temper. You need to maintain control, and this only makes the call more emotional.
- Suggest your customer is being dishonest. There are many reasons for getting behind, and most are understandable. Give him or her the benefit of the doubt.
- Be inflexible. Most situations can be resolved, but compromise is necessary. Without it, you face an all-or-nothing situation. That increases the chances of losing a customer.
- Threaten your customer. In addition to creating potential legal problems, you'll almost surely alienate your client.

Whether you are collecting money your company has rightfully earned, resolving conflicts or problems for your customer or prospecting new customers, some basic concepts need to be remembered. If getting business, keeping business and profiting in business were easy, you wouldn't be needed. Always remember that your customer may not make you happy, but the customer is the reason you are here. The customer pays your salary.

No business truly functions until something is sold. Likewise, no business stays successful for long without attention to customers — both serving them and managing them when necessary. The telephone has become a key factor in customer service and accounts receivable. The next chapter focuses on tips for the telemarketer who wants to increase sales and improve profits.

7

YOUR TELEMARKETING PRESENTATION

As a company representative you are also a telemarketer. You "sell" the company and yourself each time you make a cold call, arrange an appointment or ask for a collection. You may also be in a position to advance company sales. The intentional telemarketer has additional skills that the accidental or situational telephoner often lacks. Anyone who conducts business over the telephone can learn valuable lessons and tactics from the professional telemarketer. Concentrate on the following topics to maximize the power of your presentation each time you speak with a customer on the phone.

Gain Your Customer's Agreement

You have now determined that your customer is no longer a suspect, or someone who may use your product; he or she is a genuine prospect who does use your product or one similar to it.

Therefore, it is worth your time to persuade him or her to buy your product:

- Summarize the important points of your fact-finding with your customer. Even though you think you heard everything correctly, you may be mistaken on a critical point.
- Get your customer agreeing with you. This is the other benefit of summarizing the information you uncovered in probing. As you relate accurate information back to your customer, his or her natural reaction is to agree. This "softens up" the customer, who gets in the habit of saying yes or agreeing with you. An excellent technique for accomplishing this is to start with a confirming question. For example, "Do you agree the dependability of these pumps is probably more important to your customers than a slightly higher price?"
- Look for your customer's "hot button." If you have done a good job of probing — and you need to in order to make a strong presentation — you have probably discovered several needs your customer has that you can satisfy. However, some of these needs are more important than others.
- You may *think* you know what's important, but you could be totally wrong. Ask customers to list their needs according to their importance. You not only get customers to tell you what they think is most important, but you also get them involved in working toward a solution. This further commits them subconsciously.

Use Benefits

You have now identified the problem that is the most important to your customers, and you have them agreeing with you. Now is the time to present your solution to their problem or need.

To maximize your effectiveness and be most persuasive, you

need to explain your solution in terms of how it will help or benefit their business. Put yourself in the role of an assistant buyer for that company. Why would you buy it? Never forget the difference between features or characteristics of a product and the benefits it provides to the user. Benefits sell.

Always be willing to educate your customers on new applications or uses for your product or service. Remember, you are a specialist and your customers use many different products and services. They may not even be using them in the most efficient or profitable way for their business. By showing new uses for your product, you become part of their business. And that gives you a competitive advantage.

Speaking of competition, make sure you can compare your product or service to the competition if asked. Of key importance are two things:

1. **Compare Apples to Apples.**
   Is cost a fair comparison if one product lasts substantially longer than another? Probably not. Useful life and the cost associated with that becomes a comparison.

   Example: Brand X light bulbs last 1000 hours, but cost $1. Brand Y light bulbs last 250 hours, but cost 50 cents. To get 1000 hours of light with light bulb Y, you would spend $2. That's doubling your budget.

2. **Always Compete Fairly.**
   Your customer is studying you as well as your product or service. He or she may be very knowledgeable about it and will know if you lied or could find out. Would you buy something from someone who lied to you? Doubtful! Fight hard and compare aggressively — just do it fairly.

Let's assume that you know your product and the competition very well. What else can help you be more valuable? Be the authority on what can increase demand for your product or service. Salty nuts and beer go hand-in-hand because consumption of one increases the demand for the other. Your product or service may "partner" very well with another product. Constantly search for such a mix — it could open whole new markets. Never forget what *benefit* sells your product or service.

The Winning Presentation Formula:
Product/Service + Use = Benefit

Justify the Cost

Your customer now believes in you, and you have shown how using your product or service will improve business. Finished? Not yet. You need to help your customer build a business case for buying your product or service. He or she may have a boss watching, too. The best way to accomplish this is to cost justify or show how the dollar amount of the benefits will exceed the purchasing cost.

A key area to consider when cost-justifying the purchase is the area of business your customers consider most important. For example, if your customer told you the chief goal was to increase sales, then you should direct your cost-justifying to that objective. Be flexible. Always remember, what *you* think is important may mean nothing to your customer. Have your customer tell you what's important.

To make the process of cost-justifying easier, there are certain steps you can take:

- Determine what aspect of your customer's business you are helping. Are you helping his or her sales department by offering a new product to sell? Are you helping to control maintenance costs by selling longer-lasting light bulbs? What part of the business are you going to improve?
- Clarify exactly how you are going to help your customers. Will you increase their sales? Will you decrease their costs? It's important to know. Increasing sales may not be attractive to customers who are already at capacity in production,

warehousing and distribution. They might have to buy a million-dollar warehouse to store $50,000 worth of new products — *not* a good investment. Make sure your solutions fit your customers' plans and don't cost them more than they make.

- Translate the projected increase or decrease into dollars. For example, "My research shows a potential savings of $4,000 per year in lighting costs for your warehouse. From the numbers you gave me, you have 4,000 light bulbs you need to replace every three months. Is that right? (Get the confirmation.) If you use my long-life bulbs, you will have to replace the bulbs only once every year. Your total lighting costs would be $4,000 (at $1 each) compared to the $8,000 (at 50 cents each) you're now spending. Sound better?" (Again, get the customer to agree.)
- Finally, compare the benefits your customer will enjoy to the cost of your solution.
- Our light bulb example illustrates this. Even though your customer pays $1 per light bulb, which is twice as much as what he or she is currently paying, the *real gain* is less cost in replacing bulbs. The total process looks like this:

    - Customer need: lower maintenance costs
    - Department: maintenance
    - Your goal (what you can effect): decrease maintenance costs through light bulb purchases
    - How? by having the customer purchase your bulbs, which are changed only once in two years instead of four times a year

    Purchasing your light bulbs also reduces labor costs because less time is spent changing light bulbs. Get those figures from your customers to involve them in solving their problems.

From your fact-finding with your customer and by using this technique, you not only solve a problem, but justify the expense. Here are some key things to remember:

1. Identify and confirm your customers' needs.
2. Get a qualified picture of their current situation.
3. Show them the profit potential with your product or service.

It takes practice, but after you have used this technique a few times, you'll be able to quickly identify the hot issues and key numbers that will make your presentation much stronger.

How to Handle Sales Objections

Every incoming and outgoing call is a potential sales call. Every sales presentation and every salesperson meets with objections from customers. You have to deal with objections. The key to dealing with them successfully is to anticipate them and have a valid answer ready. Basically, there are five types of objections:

1. **Request for Information**
   Your customer may just need some information clarified.

2. **Price Objections**
   This could be a question of value to the customer or a stall technique.

3. **Personal Objections**
   The person may have a bias against you because of race, sex, religion, etc. He or she may also distrust you because of something that happened in the past. Signs of this can be silence, sarcasm or open hostility.

4. **Approval**
   This may be the person who was delegated to examine, research and make recommendations to a superior about your product or service. It could, however, be a person who

assumed the job and doesn't have much authority. Either way, you won't be able to close the sale immediately. Be patient, but determine quickly if this person can sign the contract or can influence the decision-maker. If not, determine who can, and approach that person.

Sample Objections and What They Mean

Price objections are the most common and the toughest objections to deal with. The customers and territories you deal with are all competitive and demanding. Add the fact that most of your buyers are experienced, and you have a very risky situation to neutralize. Your ability to answer this objection in a positive style can be the difference between closing or losing the sale.

Here are some key questions to ask yourself in dealing with price objections:

1. Is price really your customer's main objection?
2. How badly does your customer need your product or service?
3. How serious is the customer's resistance to price?
4. Is your customer telling the truth?
5. Is your customer trying to get a "low ball" price to bargain with your competition?
6. Is the customer ethical?
7. Will the customer buy if the price is right?

Here are some guidelines to use in dealing with price objections:

1. **Know Your Buyers and Their Needs.**
   The more you know about your customers and their needs, the more you can personalize your approach to handle their price objections.

2. **Anticipate Price Resistance.**
   Keep track of the common objections and even some of the uncommon ones. You may want to break them down by

customer or industry. This preparation pays off.

3. Talk Savings.
If your product is priced higher than the competition's, speak in terms of saving dollars because of higher quality and the need to buy less frequently.

4. Approach Your Customer's Practical and Realistic Side.
You get what you pay for. Customers who buy a product or service at a ridiculously low price know that something isn't right. They'll get less service or poor warranty support later.

5. Make Sure Your Customers Know the Risks They Are Taking.
If they are existing customers, make sure they realize they're sailing into uncharted waters. They know what they'll get from you. The new company may not guarantee what you can.

6. Convince Your Customers That You Offer a Better Value.
Don't bad-mouth your competition — just sell the quality and benefits of your products or services. The more benefits you discuss, the easier it becomes for your customers to draw their own conclusions — hopefully positive — about you and your product or service.

7. Make Yourself an Added Value.
Distinguish yourself from your competition by doing extra things for your customers — things that a lower-priced competitor can't compensate for. Treat their businesses like your own. Call them and suggest ideas to reduce costs or make their jobs easier. These are pluses that lower prices can't fight.

8. **Don't Get a Reputation for Being "Easy."**
You need your customers' respect to keep their loyalty. Cutting your price can lead to the feeling that you don't have confidence in your product or service and its ability to stand on its own merit. This leads to a dangerous spiral of always reducing prices. Be proud of your product or service.

One technique to use is the half-price question. Ask your customers if they would buy your product or service at half the original price. If they agree to buy, you can answer with something like, "Now I'll show you enough benefits to make it worth a fair price." In the majority of cases, however, they won't even take it at half price. This could be for one of two reasons:

1. High price is usually the first objection used — generally to get rid of the easily discouraged. It's almost an automatic reaction and not meant sincerely.
2. Customers need more information. They probably don't have enough knowledge about your product or service and how they will benefit from its use. This is your chance to educate them and, at the same time, sell them!

Here are some other types of objections:

- "Send me some information." This person is probably too busy or has no interest at this time.

- Procrastination. To deal with this objection effectively, you need to determine what motivates your buyer.

Here are some typical motivations for buyers:

1. **Recognition**
About 50 percent of buyers fit in this category. They want approval from others. The strategy for dealing with these people should be to stress company and product or service

prestige.

2. Security
Another 25 percent of your buyers need security. They don't like risks. They have to believe that your product or service will be risk-free. To deal with this type of buyer, be sure to stress dependability and limited risks.

3. Achievement
The last 25 percent fit in this category. These buyers are looking for gain. To appeal to them, concentrate on increased performance or higher profit with your product or service.

Your key strategy in dealing with your customers is to determine if they have a *desire for reward* or a *desire to avoid pain.* By determining which desire has priority, you can appeal to their stronger motivation and seriously reduce the chance of procrastination. To do this, you have to listen very carefully to what your customers emphasize.

Here are some hints on how to appeal to each one of these styles:

1. Recognition-Needers
- Relate a successful sales story of another customer.
- Use references (other customers' names) to add credibility.
- Be ready with other customers' opinions.
- Make sure your customer knows that you and your product or service can do what nobody else can.

2. Security-Needers
- Sell the quality of your product or service and your company. Also make sure you convince your customer of your own credibility.
- When dealing with a competitive situation, stress positive comparisons favoring your product or service. Don't speak negatively about your competition.
- Use examples of unsuccessful uses. For example, "XYZ company tried to use lighter-weight shingles, but they

didn't last long."

3. **Achievers**
   - Be open with your customers. Don't disguise issues. Face them head on.
   - Speak to your customers in terms of performance. They want to know the bottom line.
   - Talk price when asked. This may be an area where you even need to cut price a little.

By determining what motivates your customers and how you can press their "hot buttons," your chances for success increase greatly.

Answering Formats

Once you determine what type of objection you're dealing with, you need to address it with a strong, convincing answer. There are many ways of answering objections, but here are some of the most successful:

1. **Set Up (If...then)**
   You verbally set a contract with your customer.
   Objection: "Your price is too high."
   Answer: "If I could show you how using my light bulbs would actually save you money, would you try some?"

2. **FFF (Feel, Felt, Found)**
   Agree with your customer, show support from other businesses and describe their discoveries.
   Objection: "Your price is too high."
   Answer: "I understand how you *feel*, and many of my customers *felt* the same way. What they *found*, though, was that my light bulbs lasted 20 percent longer, which actually saved them

money over light bulbs that were 10 percent less expensive."

3. **Question**
Actually repeat their objections back to them. This helps you understand the real reason behind their objections.
Objection: "Your price is too high."
Answer: "My price is too high? Too high compared to what?"

4. **Reverse**
Reverse their objections.
Objection: "Your price is too high."
Answer: "Actually, I think _____ 's price is too high."
Objection: "What do you mean?"
Answer: "Since my light bulbs last 20 percent longer than the competition, mine should be 20 percent higher. Instead they're only 10 percent higher, so you actually save money."

5. **Deny**
Openly deny the customer's statement.
Objection: "Your price is too high."
Answer: "No, it's not."
Objection: "Why not?"
Answer: "Because my light bulbs last 20 percent longer for only 10 percent more money. You're really saving money."

A note of caution. Be very careful to avoid sounding argumentative here. It's best if you are familiar with your customer when you use this one.

6. **Admit**
Actually agree with your customers — but only partially.
Objection: "Your price is too high."
Answer: "Yes, my price is 10 percent higher. However,

when you consider that my bulbs last 20 percent
longer, I'm really the best buy available."
7. **Explain**
Justify why your product is worth the extra cost.
Objection: "Your price is too high."
Answer: "Let me explain why I'm 10 percent higher. We
use a special, longer-lasting filament that costs
more to produce. However, our bulb will last
20 percent longer, so you save in the long run."

The Challenge of Objections

1. Objections are an inevitable and essential part of selling.
2. You must control your emotions when answering objections.
3. Many objections are really excuses to cover the fact that your
customer hasn't been convinced that he or she has a good
reason to buy.
4. If your customer changes objections under pressure, he or
she reveals hollow excuses — not real objections.
5. When those changes occur, you should retreat and find out
more about his or her needs.
6. Your customers may have one or several legitimate objections.
Often, though, these need to be refined into something more
specific. After their objections have been isolated, it is
generally best if you convert them to questions before
answering.
7. Your answers must be adjusted according to whether your
customers' objections are general or specific.
8. Specific objections will apply to your product or service.
Technical specifications, performance capabilities and service
contracts are examples of specific objections. These are
generally answered by being knowledgeable about your
product or service.
9. Universal objections, however, generally deal with price and
competition. These need to be answered by increasing your

customers' perceptions of the value and quality of your product or service.

10. Whenever your customer has agreed that his or her objection has been answered, it could mean that he or she is ready to buy. At this point, you should try to close.

11. Always confirm that you have answered your customer's objection to his or her satisfaction. Use simple confirmation techniques such as "Fair enough," "Does that make sense to you," and "Is that agreeable to you?"

12. Remember, if there were no objections, salespeople wouldn't be needed. If your company weren't in the business of selling something, you wouldn't be employed there. No matter what position you have, you are a sales representative for your company. You are needed to handle objections.

Common Sales Problems and Mistakes

Throughout this book, you have seen ways to positively, proactively and consciously structure your telephone presentations to maximize your chances for success. If you follow these steps, you will see your success increase dramatically. However, there's one area that still needs to be covered — that black hole known as mistakes. Sometimes even a little mistake can undo all the good you did up to that point. Therefore, knowing what *NOT* to do becomes as important as knowing *WHAT* to do. Here are some of those pitfalls:

Five Death Sentences to a Sale

Although many things can go wrong in any sales presentation, there are five mistakes that show up most often. These are five mistakes that can kill your presentation or doom it before it even gets started. Memorize them and avoid them at all costs.

1. **Not Reaching the Right Person**

   All too often, a salesperson will talk to the first person who listens. Even if that person *wants* to help, he or she may not have the authority to make any commitments. Unfortunately, this is generally discovered when the salesperson tries to close and hears "I need to take this to..." or "You'll have to talk to...." Be sure to qualify the person you're talking to. Can he or she make the decision? If not, who can? It saves a lot of sales time to find out up front.

Not everyone is the decision-maker, but some people can block you from getting to the decision-maker. Even though these people slow you down, you have to work with them. There are also people with influence that can kill your sale if they want to. It sometimes takes a little "politicking" to include these people in your process, but it pays off.

2. **Talking About Features Instead of Benefits**
The second death sentence occurs for one of two reasons: excessive enthusiasm or ignorance of your customer and his or her needs. Features enable a customer to enjoy a product or service's benefit, but a feature by itself doesn't mean anything. Many companies talk about the new enhancements to Model X. But salespeople have to translate these features into benefits for customers and prospects. You may know how a feature will benefit your customer, but don't assume he or she knows. CONFIRM IT! Spell it out in the customer's language, not yours.

3. **Winning Arguments**
All of us have at some time regretted what we said. It may have been in anger, or it may have just been a mistake. Nowhere is it more costly than in sales. Even if your customer is difficult to deal with or upsets you with some careless or thoughtless remark, don't jeopardize the sale for a few minutes' satisfaction by starting an argument or making an emotional point. Control your emotions. As the saying goes, "Don't win the battle and lose the war." Your customer has the final say — so make sure it's "yes."

One point of caution here. YOU have to be the judge of when that customer is being difficult and when he or she is infringing on your rights. If you don't stand up for your own integrity, nobody else will, either.

4. **Not Asking for the Sale**
   People rarely tell each other, particularly strangers, how they want to be treated, but they demonstrate it. Your customer may have listened to your whole presentation, objected a few times and is now satisfied that your product or service will satisfy his or her need. Will he or she ask to buy it? Hardly! Since the majority of our communication involves signs and signals, that is probably how you will be informed. *Your customer lets you know it's okay to ask for the sale.* If you don't ask, your customer won't volunteer to buy. What's more, he or she will lose interest or confidence in you as you continue to avoid the close. All too soon, you've talked yourself out of a sale without ever asking.

5. **Talking Too Much**
   The last death sentence ties in very closely with not asking. Some salespeople mistake silence for acceptance. As long as the customer is quiet, they keep talking. What may actually be happening is that the customer is waiting for his or her chance to signal the salesperson to close. As the salesperson talks on, that "window of opportunity" begins to close and the customer begins to cool off. Soon, the customer has lost all interest or may even feel irritated about wasting time. Be aware of the buying signals discussed earlier and always be willing to ask for the sale. If the customer says "no," it's your opportunity to remove whatever objection he or she may have. Respond to a few "no's," and the only answer left is "yes."

The Most Common Mistakes

The Five Death Sentences almost always result in a lost sale. However, there are other mistakes a salesperson can make that create trouble or failure. Although they may not be quite as serious, they should be avoided. Here are four of the most common:

- **Dropping the Price**
  Many salespeople think that lower prices automatically mean higher demand and more sales. This is not the case. More often than not, price is associated with a quality product or service and its perceived value. When customers say, "Your price is too high," they're generally asking for more information about the value of your product or service. By automatically dropping your price, you send a signal back that says: 1) My product isn't as good as I said it was; 2) Since I was wrong on #1, I may be wrong on other things I told you. Now you have two credibility problems — one with your product or service and one with you. This creates a hole that's almost impossible to dig out of. You're better off sticking to the value of your product or service.

- **Announcing Instead of Selling**
  If you are very knowledgeable about your product or service (and you should be), you can be guilty of making that deadly assumption: thinking that your customer can translate new features of your product or service into new benefits for his or her business. When you make that assumption, you just announce the new features rather than start the new sales process.

  The process has to start from scratch every time. Your customer is not the expert on your product or service — you are. Make sure he or she knows how those new features are going to help his or her business. And don't take his or her understanding for granted. Your sales presentation must be easy to understand in order to be effective.

- **Hard-Selling Instead of Need-Selling**
  We all have an image in our minds of the fast-talking, hard-sell salesperson that nobody wants to talk to. There may have been a place for that type of personality once, but there

isn't now. Today's customers are more educated, more sophisticated and less likely to be intimidated or convinced by that style. They are looking for salespeople who respect their wishes, who are a reputable source of information, who can help them with their problems and needs and who have their business success as a top priority. In return, they will place their orders where they feel most secure.

Be a part of their business and appeal to their needs. Your odds of success are much better this way. If you don't believe this is true, look at all the customer service 800 numbers available today. Companies have realized that taking care of needs — from how to cook a turkey to how to clean grape juice off carpet — is more important than the old hard-sell approach. Solve your customers' problems, and you'll make a sale.

- **Failure to Follow Up**
  By now it should be clear that every customer should be treated as a special person. One of the key ways that salespeople can distinguish themselves from "the herd" is by following up. This means several things to the salesperson eager to succeed. Following up on delivery or installation of your product or service does several things. It ensures that everything went the way it was supposed to, which is a key concern of your customer. If not, you have a chance to remedy the problem before it escalates into a bigger problem. Equally important is the message you send to your customer:

  1. You're professional and make sure all commitments are met.
  2. You care about your customer's welfare. This alone separates you from your competition and gives you a long-term competitive edge.

Follow-up doesn't have to stop there. If you have a "tickler file," a day-by-day record of special events coming up, you can make sure your customer is recognized on occasions such as birthdays and anniversaries. This personalization is rarely practiced but pays big dividends.

Some Final Dos and Don'ts

There are some dos and don'ts that need to be mentioned as a final note. These are little things that add up to the overall impression you leave your customer:

1. **Returning Calls**

   This is an obvious courtesy, but it's amazing how many people are lax about returning calls and how much irritation they create. Make sure you return a call as promised. For example, you promise to call back by 4 p.m. with a delayed-shipment update. Even if you don't have any new information, call back by 4 p.m. and remind your customer you're calling back, as promised. What your customer remembers is that you kept your promise.

2. **Being Afraid to Say, "I Don't Know, but I'll Find Out"**

   No customer expects you to know the answer to every question, but he or she does expect honesty at all times. If you don't know, say so and then get the answers for your customer.

3. **Non-Sales Activity**

   Very few things irritate a customer more than being ignored when he or she needs some non-sales support. Too many salespeople don't have anything to do with their customers unless it generates an immediate order. Customers are not stupid. They will see through phoniness and very likely will place their orders with someone else. Help your customer as much as you reasonably can, and your customer will help you with orders.

4. **Remembering the "Little" People**
   Don't forget courteous greetings to receptionists and secretaries, and remember their names, taking notes if you need to. They may be the key influence to their bosses, or they may be the screeners for your opportunities. One company lost a $300,000 account because the receptionist was moved to a different job and couldn't screen the competition any more.

5. **Getting Angry If Your Customer Doesn't Buy**
   There may be many reasons why your customer doesn't buy when you want him or her to. It's your job to find out why and to try to change his or her mind. Remember, nobody closes every sale. If you get angry or upset, though, you seriously hurt your chances for closing future sales. Control your feelings — you'll have another chance. Stay positive, work your plan and win the next one.

8

CLOSING TECHNIQUES

When we talk to people face to face, there are natural and logical times to end the conversation. On the telephone, however, we don't have the visual cues that play a major role in how we interact with the other person. That's why sometimes it's a struggle to end a phone conversation; we're not sure how to end it without making the other party feel uncomfortable.

It is important to remember two things:

1. You are capable of maintaining control of the conversation regardless of whether you initiated it.
2. Ending a phone conversation doesn't have to be awkward. You can be straightforward without upsetting or hurting the caller's feelings.

REGULAR BUSINESS
Here are some tips on how to end phone conversations:

1. **Seek a Smooth Transition.**
   Abruptly ending a telephone conversation is as bad as failing

to close it in a straightforward manner. If you abruptly end a conversation, callers wonder what they said to cause your change in behavior. They invariably assume what they said produced a negative reaction.

Plan ahead. Give yourself time to close a conversation gradually. Don't wait until you have to go to a meeting to let the caller know it's time to hang up.

2. **Don't hesitate.**
There is no doubt about it: hesitation breeds awkwardness and discomfort on the telephone. If callers sense your hesitation, regardless of what reasons you give for ending the conversation, they assume there is a problem.

When you want to end the conversation, initiate the steps outlined below in a straightforward, firm, professional manner:

a. *Summarize the conversation.*
Summarize the conversation to tell the caller it is time to conclude. Use a paraphrase-reflect-probe sequence:

- **PARAPHRASE** the conversation to assure callers you heard and understood what they said.
- **REFLECT** on the caller's mood: "Ms. Jones, does the plan meet with your approval?" or "Mr. Kent, I'm ready to begin on the project right away. Are you comfortable with the outline we've discussed?"
- **PROBE** to close the conversation. ("Mrs. Smith, now that I have this information I can collate the statistics right away.")

b. *Repeat action steps.*
It is critical to reiterate action steps you agree upon so you both have a clear understanding of what steps are to be taken and who is responsible. Repeating these

action steps can lead you to the close of the conversation:

- "So we will meet on Thursday to go over the Anderson account. I'll get started on the research right away."
- "I will have the report on your desk Friday. In the meantime, if I have questions, can I call you?"

c. *Let the other party go.*
Sometimes closing a conversation is as easy as saying:

- "Well I know you are busy. I appreciate your help."
- "Thanks for your time. The information you've given me is very helpful. I'll let you go now."

This technique not only gets you off the telephone but makes others feel as though you respect them and their time.

d. *Let the other party hang up first.*
This may sound like a small point, but letting callers actually hang up first gives them a feeling of control over the conversation. It also protects you from accidentally hanging up on the caller in the event that he or she thinks of something to say at the last minute or gives you a sales order.

Finally, letting callers hang up first means they won't hear the final "click" of being disconnected.

Telemarketing
Now that you have planned your sales presentation through introduction, probing and objections, it's time to look at some sample closes. There are two critical parts to closing:

1. Identifying buying signals
2. Closing techniques

Identifying Buying Signals
Throughout your presentation, you should be listening for buying signals. They may come shortly after you introduce yourself to your customer, they may come part way through your telemarketing presentation, or they may not come at all. Always be listening for them, though. What are these signals?

- **Silence**
  Generally this will not be a buying signal if it happens early in the call. Your customer may be waiting for you to prove you have something worth his or her time. However, if you have gone through a presentation, answered several objections and hear silence on the other end of the line — go for the close. That silence may be telling you that you have answered all objections and he or she is ready to say "yes."

- **Questions**
  Questions like "How soon can it be installed?" or "What do I need for my equipment room?" tell you that your customer may have made the decision to buy and is ready to purchase. Questions about delivery schedules, installations and post-buying activities also indicate a desire to buy. If the customer sounds doubtful or cool when asking these questions, look out. You may need to answer an objection first.

- **Reference of Ownership**
  If you hear your customer say something like, "I can use that on the project I'm starting next month," or "I can really take care of my big account with that," try closing. Your customer is telling you that your product will help him or her. Confirm these feelings by asking for the sale. Remember, since you can't see his or her face you have to get your signal from listening.

- **Small Details**
  When your customer starts talking about small details concerning your product, he or she may be ready to say "yes." "I wonder which color will work best?" and "Should we run ads on the eight ounces or 12 ounces first?" are examples of small-detail questions. Resist the temptation to get caught up in answering these and close the sale first.

Proven Closing Techniques

Once you have identified the signal that your customer is ready to close, you need to complete the sale. More sales are lost by failing to ask for the sale than for any other reason. There are many ways of asking for the sale, but these are the most effective:

1. **The Direct Close**
   Here you ask directly for the business. For example, "Will you buy?" or "Can I write you up?" For straightforward, no-nonsense customers, this is often the best approach. Be as direct as they are. With this close, however, you have a 50-percent chance of getting a "no."

2. **The Assumptive Close**
   This is where you assume the customer has made up his or her mind to buy your product or service and only needs to work out some of the minor details. An example of this is: "Do you want the red desk or would you prefer the white?" This closing technique removes the emotional burden of making the big choice and is often very effective with less aggressive buyers.

3. **The Forced Choice Close**
   This close gives your customer a choice of products or services. For example, "What's the best size — 12 ounces or 16 ounces?" Although the forced choice is very similar to the assumptive close, the forced choice gives the decision to buy to your customer. You 're just offering two choices.

4. **The Guarantee or Incentive Close**

This offers an inducement to your customer to act either with security or haste. An example of this close is: "If you act now, you can lock in this price before the increase next week," or "If you buy now and don't like it, you can return it in 30 days for a full refund."

5. **The Narrative Close**

If you hear a hesitation on the other end, bring up a situation that involves another customer and your product or service. For example, "XYZ Company didn't use our light bulbs either. Since they started, though, they've saved six to eight thousand dollars per year in maintenance costs."

6. **The Summary Close**

This is the close where you summarize your telemarketing presentation, emphasizing the benefits. After you have reviewed the benefits, your closing statement should sound something like this: "Ms. Jones, considering all these benefits, is there any reason why you can't order now?"

7. **The Call-Back Close**

You can use this if you are forced into a call-back situation. This helps you fight the "let me think about it" objection. When you do call your contact back, open by apologizing for forgetting to tell him or her something. Also add that it's important. After you have explained that new piece of information, review your main benefits from your earlier presentation, this time adding "as you remember we agreed," etc. In short, repeat the process. The key point to remember here is DON'T ASK YOUR CUSTOMER IF HE OR SHE HAS THOUGHT ABOUT IT.

8. **The "Why Not?" Close**

If you have answered all your customer's obvious objections and he or she still isn't receptive to your normal closing techniques, try this approach: "Mr. _____ , you obviously have some reason for not buying. Would you help me out and tell me why you won't buy?"

No close works 100 percent of the time. Similarly, not every customer gives you clear buying signals. But by being aware of signals and using these techniques, your chances for success increase dramatically. One last word of caution: Once you have asked for the sale, be quiet. More salespeople have talked themselves out of sales than have won a customer with extra "jabbering." Let silence work for you. After you have asked, it's the customer's responsibility to answer.

Remember that your close creates an impression in your customer that lasts until your next contact. Keep that impression positive to ensure repeat business.

9

TAKING BETTER MESSAGES

Taking messages is one of the most vital functions of telephone professionals. Unclear, inaccurate or incomplete messages result in lost sales, angry customers and, even worse, an angry boss. Perhaps when all offices have voice mail, we won't need to take messages. But until then, telephone message-taking is here to stay.

Here are five ways you can take messages more effectively:

1. **Get Complete Information.**
   This may sound basic, but far too many telephone messages are incomplete. They lack complete names, accurate telephone numbers, the name of the caller's business and what response, if any, the caller expects.

   Some of the worst errors are made when we rely solely on the caller's message without asking for details. For instance, leaving a message for your boss that says "Call your sister" can lead to confusion. What if your boss has two sisters? How does he or she know whom to call?

To avoid these pitfalls, define the information you need from every caller. This should include:

- Name (first *and* last)
- Company or organization
- Telephone number, including area code if necessary
- Purpose of call
- Desired response (return the call, caller will call back, etc.)
- Any special information (call back after 2 p.m., for instance)
- Time of call

Consistently get this information. If a caller is unwilling to cooperate, explain that it will be difficult to return the call without complete information.

Don't forget to record the time the call came in. This provides a great deal of subtle information to your boss or whoever needs to return the call. It lets him or her know several things:

- How promptly a call was returned if it was one that he or she may have made earlier in the day
- How long a customer has been waiting to get information or place an order
- How to appropriately return calls made from different time zones

2. **Spell Names Accurately.**
   If you have any doubt about the spelling of a caller's name, ask. Don't feel embarrassed. The caller will be flattered you took the time to get it right.

If the name has an unusual pronunciation, clarify it with the caller, then note the phonetic pronunciation so the person returning the call can be accurate.

Listen closely to the caller's words. Is it Bruce Brown? Or Mr. Bruce Brown? Or Mr. Brown? Indicating this on a message can be of tremendous help to the person returning the call. It helps him or her address the caller appropriately, either informally or formally. In these circumstances, you need to listen with your "third ear." You will be able to hear how the caller likes to be addressed.

If you address someone incorrectly, apologize and make note of the correct name and title; then go on with the conversation.

3. **Avoid Telephone "Tag" Games.**
We've all experienced this frustration. Messages are left. You return the call but the person you want to reach isn't in. Then he or she calls back, but you're not available...and on and on.

You can minimize telephone tag by the message you take:

- Tell callers when the individual they are trying to reach will be available: "Mr. Jones is usually in the office from 1 p.m. to 2 p.m." Suggest they call back at that time.
- Ask when it is a good time to reach them.

This simple step saves everyone, including you, a lot of time and energy and once again reinforces your professional image.

4. **Volunteer to Help.**
If someone calls for your boss or another person in the organization who isn't available, ask the caller if there is anything you can do to help. This does two things: it gives

you information on the purpose of the call, and it may eliminate the necessity of your boss's returning the call. Even if you can't help, the information may still be valuable to the person who must return the call.

Here is a good example of how you can save valuable time:

CALLER: "Is Mrs. Grant in?"

YOU: "Yes, but she will be in meetings most of the day. May I give her a message or perhaps help?"

CALLER: "Well, I am calling about the job your company advertised. I'm interested in applying for it."

YOU: "Mrs. Grant is currently taking resumes for that position. Let me give you her full name, title and address, and you can mail it to her today."

Mrs. Grant will appreciate this because you saved her an unnecessary interruption, since she would have told the caller the same thing. The caller is pleased because he or she got the desired information and the opportunity to take immediate action. Finally, you saved yourself time because the job applicant won't have to call back to reach Mrs. Grant.

If you anticipate receiving a large number of calls for a job opening, you might offer to conduct this type of screening for the personnel director. Ask him or her to give you basic information about the status of the position or where the company is in its hiring process.

5. **Evaluate the Caller's Mood.**

Indicating the caller's mood may seem strange when taking phone messages, but think about it. If you had to return a call, wouldn't you like to know if you were going to be greeted with hostility?

Indicating the caller's mood is particularly important in sales and customer service because these are situations where building and maintaining positive relationships with customers is crucial to the success of a company.

You can record the caller's mood in one of several ways depending on the time you have. You can either note significant words, phrases or attitudes or devise an attitude-rating scale from one through five (positive to negative).

If you have time and if the caller seems particularly upset, you can probe a little to get a sense of the problem. Sometimes callers will tell you without any encouragement! Whatever information you get helps the person who must return the call.

Leaving Better Messages

To leave better messages, give complete information. Reread the list for getting complete information while taking better messages. Use this as a checklist when delivering a message, too. You'll save everyone time and frustration by being complete, yet brief. Keep your message to 30 seconds. A longer message is more difficult for someone to record accurately or to listen to attentively. The more you say, the more someone can misunderstand.

Final Thoughts

People who communicate by telephone stand on the front line of most modern businesses. They greet customers, sell products, conduct meetings, confer with clients and handle a host of other vital business activities.

If you stand on this front line, your job is to listen, respond and communicate effectively. If you do your job well, you communicate much more than just facts or information about a product or service. You communicate an image of yourself and your company.

Good telephone skills make an important difference in how callers perceive your company. How you demonstrate these skills tells callers a lot about your professionalism, how well-managed your company is, its attitude toward customers and clients, its attitude toward employees and your attitude toward the company.

As you conduct business on the telephone each day, remember the messages you communicate to callers. Evaluate your effectiveness not only in terms of the overt information you give the caller but of the subtle information as well.